JERKY PEOPLE

THEIR JERKY-MAKING RECIPES, STORIES AND TIPS

Mary Bell

Jerky People / Mary Bell
ISBN 0-9653572-5-2
Library of Congress 2002101516

148 pages
Includes Index

$14.00 U.S.
$19.00 CAN

FIRST EDITION
1 2 3 4 5 6 7 8 9 10

Printed on recycled paper with soy-based ink in the United States of America.

The Dry Store Publishing Company
Route #2, Box 156B
Lanesboro, MN 55949
www.drystore.com
marytbell@drystore.com
Voice 507-467-2928
Fax 507-467-2694

Note: Check with your dehydrator, smoker or oven manufacturer for operating and maintenance assistance when making jerky.

Mary Bell's other books are *Dehydration Made Simple, Mary Bell's Complete Dehydrator Cookbook, Cutting Across Time* and *Just Jerky.*

Cover Design:
    Ira Newman
Illustrators:
    Dale Mann and Robert Foster
Editors:
    Pam Eyden and Ardie Eckart
Layout Design & Production:
    Rochelle Barnhart

A special thank you to Ray Howe for always being there to help. Thanks to Kay Winter and Donal Hefernan for their contributions. And thank you Neil Haugerud and Al Mathison for your excellent feedback.

DEDICATION

TO MY GRANDSON, HUNTER EVANS GEHRKE

Hunter was three days old when his mom and dad bundled him up, secured him in his car seat and headed off to our place for his Aunt Sal's wedding. Less than a mile from their home a deer rammed their car. After we were all assured that no one was hurt, except the deer, and we assessed the damage to the car, we looked intently at this brand new little man and commented that on his first outing he had already bagged his first deer.

Hunter with a hunk of meat and a bottle.

v

TABLE OF CONTENTS

FOREWORD

HON. MONTE B. CARLSON
FIFTH JUDICIAL DISTRICT
BURLEY, IDAHO

Making jerky is my hobby. It's my diversion from the courtroom. I find it satisfying and fulfilling to take a hunk of raw meat and make it tasty. Some of us make jerky because we are hunters. Not only do we want to consume what we kill, but we prefer venison jerky to venison chops. For over 30 years I've bow hunted deer and elk with the same loony partners and together we've turned a zillion deer and twenty-three elk into jerky. With that kind of tasting experience I think it is fair to say that I've become a pretty good judge of jerky.

Jerky has become a tradition in our family. While we were students with limited income, my wife and I practically lived on wild game. While pregnant with our first child, the smell of venison chops or steaks made her ill. Then, as well as now, she prefers her big game meat made into jerky. For three and a half decades we've been making jerky in a food dryer and more recently we use our smoker.

Ever notice that he who controls food, is king? Several years ago I convinced my nephew, who was doing nothing other than waiting for college to begin, to backpack with me into Idaho's mountain country for an archery elk hunt. This non-hunting six-foot-seven-inch lad from Kentucky became my pack mule and carried all my heavy camping equipment. All he required was a slice of jerky every now and then. Like a trained seal being fed a fish, my nephew actually packed out my bull elk, with no reward other than a constant (but obscene) amount of jerky.

Some say that jerky makers are just a little off the plumb line. I make jerky for my odd assortment of wack-o hunting pals, but I charge them one-third of the result—my ambulance chasing days die slowly. Once, while practicing law, I drove to Eastern Idaho to meet with a client in his home. The whole house was filled with smoke. Up above me, hanging from the rafters, were strips of raw meat. This guy had killed a deer and right there in his living room was making smoked jerky.

My favorite jerky recipe is the Kevin and Annie one from Mary Bell's book, *Just Jerky*. I like the blend of soy sauce and maple syrup. I have to admit that sometimes I add orange peelings to give it a little more zing. Like most jerky makers, I always look forward to trying new recipes and tinkering with exotic flavor combinations.

Just Jerky is the jerky maker's bible. Not only does it teach the art of drying hamburger (which, by the way, works perfectly well with ground sausage and ground turkey), it also explains how to make traditional and even unusual tasting jerkies. Mary encourages her readers to be creative and blend unusual flavors. No book on the market is better. Mary fields more questions, solves more problems, and delivers better information than anyone else in the crowded jerky theater. Not only does she give solid jerky making advice, she even answers e-mails when something goes wrong with a batch. I know, I've appealed to her wisdom more than once.

Now she's done it again with *Jerky People.* It is filled with great stories, more recipes for us addicts, and it's flavored throughout with good advice. Jerky people are a goofy bunch that actually enjoy making jerky in their attics, basements, kitchens, living rooms or garages —with or without food dryers, smokers, or ovens—and they even use such dangerous chemicals as liquid smoke. Jerky people experiment by smoking, marinating, grinding, drying, salting and flavoring all kinds of meat. (I've made antelope and cougar jerky.) Jerky people keep searching for that one great bite of jerky that has the perfect flavor. I judge this new book, *Jerky People,* as wonderful and I am personally grateful to all of those who shared their recipes, wisdom and advice.

—*Judge Monte B. Carlson*
The Jerky Judge

INTRODUCTION

Let's get one thing straight—the people in this book are not jerks—they are just people who like jerky. Granted, they are all characters who like to either hunt, fish, ride horseback, canoe, sail, backpack, or run a ranch, or are folks who run jerky companies.

"What's your story?" I asked each one of them. "How did you get started making jerky? What's unique or different about how you make it?"

Their answers were both fascinating and useful. These innovative and inventive jerky sages offer good advice and sound instructions along with some pretty terrific jerky recipes.

Since publication of my previous book *Just Jerky* in 1996, I've met quite a few of the people who wrote, telephoned and e-mailed me, or connected with me through my website. I've met others at the Minnesota State Fair, where every year I put in 12 long, dizzying days selling dehydrators and passing out samples of jerky.

"I have this really great jerky recipe," they'd say, and I'd quickly write it down. Some of these folks and their recipes appear in this book. Some people got so into jerky that they went pro and now market their own brands.

Knowing that some jerky recipes are coveted treasures, I was delighted at how many people were willing to share. Businesses, of course, were not as disclosing with their techniques, but were willing to give tips, suggestions and insights into the commercial jerky industry.

Jerky is big business. The U.S. Snack Food Association declared that meat snack sales reached $1.74 billion in 2000, which was a 31.7 percent increase over 1999. In 2001 sales increased 13.8 percent. Kathy Mulady, from *The Seattle Post Intelligencer* reported in an April 26, 2002, article that "Oberto, the largest jerky manufacturer, exceeded sales of $100 million." Founder Art Oberto, whose story is in this book, expects yearly growth of 10 to 15 percent in slow years and 20 to 30 percent in better years—that's a lot of jerky!

As Dean Clark, founder of HI MOUNTAIN SPICE COMPANY, pointed out, these figures do not include the money spent by people who make their own jerky.

Drawn by curiosity, unsatisfied tastebuds or mysterious inner urges, an increasing number of people are making jerky these days. The jerky market has grown to provide a vast quantity of materials and supplies. When Cabela's, one of the largest outfitters, first starting selling *Just Jerky* in their catalog they had one page of products related to jerky. In the recent catalog, their jerky-making supplies cover eight pages, featuring various smokers, dehydrators, cures, jerky guns and shooters, meat grinders and slicers, wood chunks, various oven accessories, vacuum packers, tenderizers and, of course, books.

Jerky People and *Just Jerky* compliment each other. *Just Jerky* provides the basics for making all kinds of jerky. It's loaded with "how-to" information and lots of recipes for making jerky. At the end of this book you will find "My Jerky Suggestions" which gives you some basic jerky-making instructions (and a few surprises).

If the stories and recipes in this book are not enough and you need a little more inspiration to make your own jerky, sing a little! In fact, to spur you on here are my favorite jerky tunes: Try, "Come On, Do The Jerk!" by the Miracles, or "Cool Jerk" by The Capitols, or "The Jerk" by the Larks. Then there's "Can You Jerk Like Me" by The Contours. And, of course, Rodney Crowell's tell-it-like-it-is ballad, "She Loves The Jerk."

—*Mary Bell*

A FOUNTAIN OF JERKY CREATIVITY

Dean Clark

If you're driving through the heart of Wyoming and you see a bumper sticker on the vehicle ahead of you that reads, "VEGE-TARIAN—An old Western word meaning Lousy Hunter," you might be following entrepreneur Dean Clark. Dean, president and founder of HI MOUNTAIN JERKY, gets the gold star for being a fountain of jerky creativity. He's got spices, a knife that slices, a board to hold raw meat while slicing and a scale. "You've got to have a scale to make jerky," he said. "You must weigh the meat so you can accurately measure and add spices."

As owner of the largest jerky spice company in the world, Dean knows a lot about jerky and the business of making it. "It's a growing market," he said. "We sell enough spices in one year to turn 40 millions pound of meat into jerky." The U.S. Snack Food Association reported that retail sales of jerky and beef sticks grew 20 percent in 1999 and 32 percent in 2000. That translates to $1.74 billion in sales in 2000. But that's just snack food and doesn't take into account the homemade jerky market.

Dean Clark got his start in the world of meat when he worked behind the counter of his father's meat market in the San Fernando Valley in southern California. After doing various jobs, he got into the oil business, went bust, then turned to the restaurant business. He got started in the spice business when he took his own spice blend to Griffins Laboratory in Chicago. He developed "Chef's Seasoning," which was followed by seasonings for venison, fish, hickory burger, then bacon, and marketed under the Campfire label.

"The best part was there was no competition at that time," Dean reported. "We'd found a niche and by 1991 our spice line was well-positioned for the beginning of the homemade jerky craze."

Today, he's got a new smoker oven and some exciting ideas on where he is going to put it. Soon he'll launch his plan to put "Jerky Shacks" in convenience stores and truck stops, so shop owners can pop frozen jerky into the Jerky Shack Oven and sell freshly made—perhaps still warm—jerky. Of course, Dean will also sell his frozen packs of seasoned, ready-to-dry jerky along with the ovens. He also intends to expand his line to grocery store frozen food departments.

SUGGESTION: "Think ahead," Dean advised. "The market's out there."

The jerky market has expanded since women have discovered that jerky is a high protein, low-fat snack food. Dean speculates that women will appreciate his new frozen jerky product because they will not have to do any cutting or marinating; instead it will be very easy to simply buy a box of frozen jerky, take it home and when the urge arises, bake jerky in their oven.

Dean, curious about history's secrets, was intrigued with how Native Americans, mountain men, cowboys and pioneers smoked and dried meat. "Jerky is the perfect food, it's nutritious, easy to carry and keeps pretty well in a saddlebag," said Dean. "If you stop and think about how our ancestors dried meat, first of all salt was heavy and there wasnot much room to carry much of it in a saddle bag, so they used wood smoke as a preservative.

"Do you know why it's

called "jerky?" he asked. "Because raw meat was cut with the grain—not against it. When it dries you have to yank to rip it and you can only do that if you cut it with the grain," he said. (He has also developed a cutting board to make cutting meat with the grain easier.)

"Old-fashioned jerky was soft, pliable and chewy, he said. "Why, old timers couldn't eat that hard, brittle kind you find now-a-days—they didn't have enough teeth!"

In the old days, old timers took leather straps off the back of their saddles, or the leather harness off of their buggy, or sometimes they used two leather belts. They laid the leather out flat and used it as a guide for the knife so that the fresh, raw meat would stay the same thickness."

TIP: Meat absorbs a marinade better if it's a little dry.

"To make jerky you've got to have a curing agent," Dean said. His cures contain salt, sugar, brown sugar, sodium nitrite (.85%), maple syrup, caramel color, and less than 2% glycerine to prevent caking. "We don't add any chemicals or preservatives to our spices, other than sodium nitrite and that's just a form of salt," Dean said. Each seasoning packet can be mixed with a maximum of four pounds of meat. All of his sea-soning blends contain salt, garlic and spice extracts. Hickory has smoke flavor with malto-dextrin. Cajun contains red, black, and white peppers, with dextrose, onions and sugar. Cracked Pepper 'N Garlic includes turmeric extract. Original has soy sauce powder (soy sauce, wheat, soybeans, salt), maltodextrin and less than 1% propylene glycol added to prevent caking. Hickory and mesquite are hydroscopic, meaning they draw moisture and can cake in their packages.

Dean uses the eye of round beef to make jerky, "You can use just about any lean cut of meat," he said, "even ground meat." He cuts meat in strips, $1/4$-inch thick, weighs the strips and measures

Dean Clark's new Jerky Snack Oven.

the seasonings, lays the strips out on a flat counter-top surface and liberally sprinkles the seasonings on each strip. He turns the slices over and repeats the sprinkling until all surfaces are covered. "Right away the color will change," Dean said. He puts the strips in a sealable plastic bag or any airtight container that's not metal and lets it marinate in the refrigerator for 24 hours.

When using an oven, either lay the strips right on the oven rack, or poke them with toothpicks and hang them from the rack, or use Dean's oven screens. "When using toothpicks you can get 4 to 5 pounds on a rack. Remember to leave a little area between the slices so the air can get through." Line the bottom of your oven with aluminum foil to catch drips. Set the temperature at 200 degrees. Check after one hour. The longer you leave jerky in the oven the harder and darker it gets.

To make jerky you can use your dehydrator, oven or smoker, or Dean's new Jerky Smoker Oven. It looks like a little refrigerator with a smoke box on the bottom and is a home version of his Jerky Shack Oven.

Did I mention that Dean also has a video, sausage stuffer and a meat grinder?

TIP: When using a dry cure as a marinade, dissolve the seasonings in ice water.

LINDA'S STORY

Although Linda and Dean are really different stories I've put them together because Linda uses HI MOUNTAIN as her main jerky ingredient.

While our ferrier, Doug Harrington was putting new shoes on our horses, he commented that his sister Linda Bergan, who happens to be my husband's barber, makes a great jerky.

"I have to do everything very well and very fast," Linda said hurriedly.

I'm a busy person with high standards, so I use Hi Mountain Hickory™ spice. I substitute a little of the water with other stuff, like Worcestershire or soy sauce, sometimes I've even used whiskey."

LINDA'S JERKY

1 tablespoon Worcestershire sauce
1 tablespoon soy sauce
1 teaspoon liquid smoke

3 pound boneless chuck roast

red pepper flakes

After marinating the strips for two days in the refrigerator in a covered container, she lays the strips on her dehydrator trays and sprinkles them with red pepper flakes.

TIP: Now here is Linda's real trick. When the jerky is finished she puts it in a sealable plastic bag, cuts a slice of fresh green pepper and puts it in the bag with the jerky.

When she wants jerky to taste a little hotter she cuts a fresh habanero in half and adds that to the jerky bag. "I came up with this when I dried a batch of jerky too long and it got way too hard. I thought I could add a little moisture and a little flavor and it worked," she grinned. "Now I do it all the time."

5

THE JERKY KING

Art Oberto

Art Oberto in his jerky mobile.

Art Oberto drives a "jerky mobile" and dons the title "Jerky King," and without a doubt he is Oh Boy! Oberto's main cheerleader. Art is a natural-born entrepreneur with great energy. His motto has been, "Have fun." When he drives his jerky mobile around the Seattle, Washington area promoting the company and its products, he wears a white suit with a red, white and green "Oh Boy! Oberto" tie.

"We were at home watching

7

television and saw the bat mobile. I told my wife Dorothy, 'if they can have one, we can have one, too.' So far, we've turned a '57, '58 and now a '59 Lincoln Town Car into our jerky mobiles," Art said proudly. "You've got to do things because you enjoy them." This philosophy has made Art and his family a great deal of money.

The Oberto Sausage Company was founded in 1918 by Art's father, Constantino. When Constantino died in 1943, Art was 16. He helped his mother keep the business alive by riding his bike to deliver their Italian sausage. Their business expanded immediately after they started spending $1,000 a month on advertising in the late 1960s. As they grew, they developed new products, such as jerky, sausage sticks, smoked dinner sausages, dry salami, kippered beef and pickled sausage. The company doubled its sales in 1995 by buying Curtice Burns Meat Snacks, Inc., which produced Smoke Craft and Lowrey's Beef Jerky. Oberto now employs more than 800 people to make nearly 400 products in four plants totalling 275,000 square feet of manufacturing and warehousing space. In 1998 Oberto's sales exceeded $100 million. In May 2002, the anticipated figure for the year was estimated at about $150 million.

"And I expect a 10 to 15 percent growth each year," Art said gleefully.

SUGGESTION: When packaging jerky there is what we call "jerky dust" in the bottom of our storage containers. We sell this jerky dust to chefs who use it in salads and as a seasoning and to add flavor to soups and sauces

Jerky accounts for more than half of Oberto's product line. Art explained that its popularity skyrocketed when people realized that at 97 percent lean, jerky was a good source of protein and a healthy food. "At one time beef had a bad rap, but that image has changed," Art said. "Plus we got lucky—we had the right products at the right time."

8

Although the Oh Boy! jerky marinades are corporate and family secrets, Art did talk a bit about how they make their jerky. They start with using the two top round cuts, which amounts to 30-35 pounds of meat from each cow. "We tried making reindeer jerky, but there wasn't enough meat to make it worthwhile," he said. Oberto buys beef from the United States, Australia and New Zealand.

Once the beef is trimmed, it's sliced about $1/4$-inch thick and marinated with spices for 24 hours. The flavored meat is either air dried or placed on screens to be dried and smoked at the same time. "Careful attention is paid to the temperature and humidity. Each jerky flavor has its own set formula," Art said. "If you'd take the same identical piece of meat and vary the temperature or the humidity, or change one marinating ingredient, it would come out tasting different. Once our jerky is dry it will keep almost forever, but you have to keep it dry," he said.

TIP: Always be responsive to customers. They'll tell you what they want. They might want a jerky that's softer or one that's hotter. Remember to listen.

Art shared his philosophy on business. "Our success is based on a formula," he said. "First we have to produce the best possible products, our company has to grow and the bottom line is that the numbers have to come out right. It is also extremely important that we have happy, contented employees as well as satisfied, loyal customers. If those things are taken care of, everything else takes care of itself."

Then he advised, "Regardless of what business you are in, find at least one mentor. Mentors helped me stay in business. Over the years I repeatedly heard what one of my mentors told me, 'Time is your most important commodity. Get the job done. Think lazy and don't do any more than you have to.' I've always loved that piece of advice. It has made my life and my work much more fun."

"Do you have any plans to retire?" I asked.

"I don't need to retire. I've never had a job," he chuckled. "I've always had a hobby."

ART'S FAVORITE JERKY RECIPE

"Jerky is great food to use in cooking. I am especially fond of the Spanish egg and dried beef dish that is called Machaca.

MACHACA NORTENA
Scrambled Eggs and Shredded Dried Meat

9 tablespoons shredded beef jerky
½ medium onion
3 chili peppers
⅓ cup oil
12 eggs, beaten
6 flour tortillas

Shred the dried beef into pieces no bigger than ⅛ inch. Finely chop the onion and the peppers. Lightly fry the onion in hot oil and add the peppers. Add the meat, stir and add eggs. Stir constantly. When the eggs are cooked, remove from heat, fill the tortillas and serve immediately.

GENTLEMAN JIM GOES LEGAL

Jim McGrew

After watching other guys sell "nickel bags" of jerky on the street corner, Jim McGrew, owner of Gentleman Jim's Gourmet Food, decided he'd go legal with his jerky operation. After spending $22,000 for equipment and getting a thorough education in the ways of governmental bureaucracy, at 9:47 a.m. on December 27, 2001, his dream finally came true. He got his United States Department of Agriculture (USDA) approval and now runs a federally approved manufacturing plant, where he makes a spicy jerky, a sweet jerky, a regular, a teriyaki and a pepper jerky.

His journey began when a buddy gave him a dehydrator he hadn't used. "When I took it out of the box I found a recipe for jerky, I bought a pound of meat and followed the directions. The following Saturday I shared my jerky with our sailing crew and ever since that day I've been expected to bring jerky every time we race our Morgan 30 sailboat, 'Jackal,'" he recalled.

"Human movement can be a critical factor in winning or losing a sailboat race," Jim explained. "Once we get the sails trimmed and the boat is up to speed, we adjust each crew member's position to get the maximum speed possible. After that you can't just get up and move around any time you want, and you can get pretty hungry during a 30-mile race when you can't go below to make yourself a sandwich. However, with a few sticks of jerky in your pocket, you've got a great high-protein food that satisfies when it hits your stomach."

With friends and racing buddies urging him to sell his jerky, Jim called the USDA and asked what he needed to set up a jerky business.

"You've got to have a licensed kitchen," was the reply.

"Do you have a book or a manual I can follow?" Jim asked.

"No. Each facility is different and each one requires individual attention."

"Okay. Is there a computer web site or any other source of information where I can get ideas?" Jim asked.

"No," was the reply.

"It was crazy," Jim said. "They had rules I was supposed to follow but no guidelines. I drew up a business plan and designed my processing area, but they refused to tell me what I had to include in it. I went on-line and I found the Department of Agriculture's web site, filed the papers and applied for a permit."

Jim found a space for his new facility for $1,000 a month and proceeded to build his plant, then contacted other people in the food industry to get an idea of what he had to include. He put in new white walls, a floor drain, stainless steel sinks and countertops. Then drew up an operating and sanitation plan and called his

local inspector to see if he had it in order. After looking it over, the inspector politely told him it needed more work and advised him to call a local jerky producer for assistance.

"I called the local jerky guy, explained who I was and told him what I was trying to do. I swear he almost giggled," Jim said.

"'Have you applied for your permit?' the other jerky producer asked.

'Done that,' I answered.

'Do you have your labels approved?'

"What? By whom?' I asked."

Unfortunately, Jim had already designed, printed and paid for 5,000 labels only to find out that they had to be approved by Washington, D.C. His labels became scrap paper.

But that wasn't the last of it. The new adviser asked if he had his HAACP plan approved.

"HAACP?" Jim questioned.

Jim learned that HAACP stands for Hazard Analysis and Critical Control Points and it outlines the production process from start to finish. It explains what procedures are required to prevent contamination and analyzes where a product is likely to be contaminated (by microrganisms, pathogens, foreign objects, spoilage, etc.).

"Then the guy asked, 'Do you have unlimited capital resources?'"

"My response was something like, 'Uh-oh!'" Jim recalled.

"Creating and getting my plan approved ended up being the most daunting task I've ever undertaken."

Jim persisted. He found several models on the USDA web site, adjusted his plan and called the inspector.

"At that point I realized I'd only scratched the surface. Literally, I'd have to track everything, from receiving the raw meat all the way through shipping."

He had to track the temperature of the inside of the delivery truck and the beef at the time it was received at the plant. He had to measure the temperature again when the meat was put in the cooler, when it went into the marinade, at the beginning of the

drying process, during the drying process and again when it was packaged. That's a lot of thermometers! He had to record how often he calibrated each thermometer. Batch numbers had to be assigned. He was required to have a procedure for noting when a problem arose, what he did to solve it and what was changed so the problem would not happen again.

"This took months to pull together," Jim sighed.

His first inspection was scheduled for September 2001. The inspector was impressed with the facility, but said it wasn't ready.

"It's my job to inspect, not instruct," the inspector said.

Gentleman Jim's packaged jerky.

"Your job is to figure out what you need." So Jim toured another jerky facility, made some changes in his plan and set a December date for his second inspection.

"I was told to make more changes. I had had enough," Jim recalled hotly. "I told the inspector to look around and tell me exactly what I needed to do to comply because the next time he came back, I didn't want any more surprises. I wanted my license!"

Jim had to install foot-level operating pedals on his sinks (three sinks at $400 each), put in a bathroom fan and use foam to seal off all the pipes running through the building to prevent a bug infestation. He obtained a copy of the inspection checklist and used that as his guide to make more changes.

"Finally I was ready and this time I passed inspection," Jim said. "For a brief moment I thought it was over.... But not yet—there were the labels to get approved."

Five jerky flavors meant five labels and five different approvals, which, because of governmental procedures, took a lot of time. He had to break each recipe into percentages of each ingredient, supply nutritional analyses, submit proposed sketches of each label and have each jerky analyzed for moisture content to make sure it was dry enough.

"It took a lot of faxing, adjusting to their recommendations, re-faxing, readjusting and re-faxing," he said.

Eventually, he cleared the hoops and started making and selling his jerky. Now, each week Jim buys up to 1,000 pounds of fresh London broil (top round) beef from Sam's Club. "They're consistent with their cuts," he said. "Plus I like the way top round holds up in a marinade."

Jim hand-slices his meat. "No machine will ever cut it," he said emphatically. "I like the rugged look of the finished jerky that you only get when meat is hand sliced. It can't be too thick, too long or too wide."

Single handedly, Jim cuts about 50 pounds an hour, then puts the slices in marinating tubs that are refrigerated for 24 hours. "I don't use any preservatives in my marinades other than what's in soy sauce. I chop fresh onions, mash fresh garlic and use the highest quality seasonings I can find."

While one batch marinates, he takes the previous day's batch and loads his dehydrators. "Each dehydrator is on a timer, which makes my job a little easier." After six and a half hours at a temperature of 160 degrees the jerky is finished. He lets it cool, weighs it, slips a toothpick into the bag, then vacuum-packs into 4-ounce packages and attaches a label.

"Between racing sailboats and making jerky, I don't have

time for a girlfriend," he said. "Believe me, after all of this I understand why guys sell nickel bags of jerky on the street."

TIP: To make good jerky always start with good quality meat and ingredients. And don't be afraid to experiment with ingredients and various drying processes. I've never had anyone give me back any of my jerky and say they didn't like it.

SWEET JERKY
1½ cup light brown sugar
½ cup clove honey
½ cup soy sauce
½ cup Worcestershire sauce
½ cup raw minced onions
2 tablespoons lime juice
1 tablespoon fresh minced garlic
1 teaspoon chili powder

2 pounds beef strips

Mix the ingredients, then add strips, coat evenly and marinate 24 hours in a covered container in the refrigerator and dry.

RUM JERKY
Jim makes this special recipe for his sailing buddies.

¾ cup of Captain Morgan™ or Myers Rum™
¾ cup light brown sugar
½ cup soy sauce
½ cup Worcestershire sauce
½ cup raw minced onions
2 tablespoons lime juice
1 tablespoon fresh minced garlic
½ teaspoon chili powder

2 pounds meat strips

Mix together the ingredients, then add strips and marinate 24 hours in a covered container in the refrigerator and dry

MOTHER'S JERKY: THE COST OF INVENTION

Sean Broadnax

Sean Broadnax is a tenacious Irishman from northern California who invented a Mother's 2-Hour Jerky Maker. His story reveals what it takes to take an idea all the way and to make it pay.

His Teflon™-coated, aluminum jerky maker is 14^1/$_2$ inches long, 8 inches wide and when folded open it stands 8 inches high. The folding top has holes for seven skewers. To make jerky, you poke strips of marinated meat with the skewers, then lock the skewers in the top holes so that the meat strips hang straight down. You put the whole contraption in a preheated 190 oven and two hours later you've got homemade jerky! It's simple and it works, although, depending on the size of the meat strips, it may take more than two hours.

Sean got the idea for this clever gadget in a flash. He was talking to a friend who told him that her mother made beef jerky by hanging it on a line out of doors. Instantly he imagined a metal rack that could be used to make jerky in an oven. He became obsessed with trying to recreate the image. It was the beginning of his long, long quest.

"Since that first day, I've been married to this product," he said. After experimenting with 20 batches of jerky, Sean saw how the jerky maker could be improved. "I got excited thinking about how much money I was

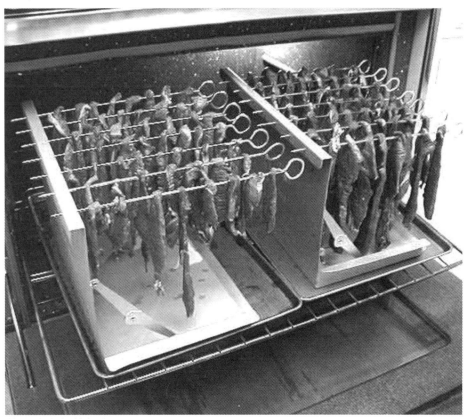
Mother's Jerky Maker in oven.

going to make," he chuckled. "I thought success would happen in a matter of months!" He took a long pause. "I was in for a big surprise."

To protect his invention he used a patent marketing company that charged him $10,000. "They got my patent, #5996820, but their fee included finding a manufacturer and they never came through with that," he said. "If I ever do this again, I'll just hire a patent attorney."

Since the very beginning Sean worried about where the money would come from to pay for everything. He worried about marketing and improving his invention. He worried about how to create the art work and about making the label decisions. He fretted over developing the user instructions and about which recipes to use. It took time to create the right packaging and everything cost more than he thought it would. During all this time he wondered if people would really like and use his invention.

Just when he thought he had his ducks in a row, he sat down and turned on his television set. "Tears of pain rolled from my eyes as I watched Ron Popielle make beef jerky with a dehydrator. I was shattered!" he recalled. "I thought it was all over and for the next six months I never mentioned the word jerky. Then a friend handed me the instruction manual for the Popielle dehydrator and I read that it made jerky in 10 to 12 hours. Instantly, I was excited since my invention takes only two hours. I was back in business!"

While his patent was pending, Sean lived in his mother's garage, manufactured jerky makers and looked around for another manufacturer. After talking with quite a few—70!—he found a Janesville, Wisconsin, company that agreed to produce his jerky maker. The owner made 560 units and not only extended him credit, but drove the units to California just in time for Sean to market them at the Yuba-Sutter County Fair.

There, the proud inventor put a propane oven on his booth table along with his jerky maker. "But people thought I was selling the oven instead of the jerky maker," he laughed. "After selling 80 units I didn't make enough to cover my costs, since each unit cost me $13 and sold for $20."

Then—smart, lucky or just plain desperate—he called the local newspaper. When the story came out, a kitchen store ordered 20 and sold them out right away. This was good news. The bad news was that the store paid $12 per unit, but they still cost him $13 to produce.

Things finally started to click when a kitchen product distributor got hold of the jerky maker and distributed it to dozens of California stores. Then Cannella Response Television, an infomercial company, decided to promote it and ordered 6,000 units. Although the first infomercial targeted the wrong audience—women and children, instead of men—things have looked up ever since.

Now, with an internet site (listed in the index at the end of this book), the infomercial and his product in stores, Sean's business has taken off. In December 2001 he sold over 5,000 units, 700 of which he personally sold and shipped from his new two-room office/apartment. After a decade of dedication, he hopes to pay his debts and take some time off from his day job at the newspaper.

"This has been the craziest time," his voice cracked. "My mom was there for me all through this. Then the week before Christmas, cancer took her. Mother's Jerky Maker was named for her."

He was quiet.

"Sometimes I wonder what's been the real cost of making this happen," he confessed.

"Let's hope lots of people make some great jerky," I said.

"Me too," he said softly.

MOTHER'S JERKY MAKER INSTRUCTIONS

Sean prefers London broil "because it has the perfect texture." he said. He cuts strips of any meat, poultry or fish about ⅛-inch thick and no longer than 8 inches. Then he marinates the strips in the refrigerator for one hour. During the marinating process he uses a fork to poke the strips several times to help the marinade penetrate faster. "Remember to remove the top rack when you preheat the oven to 200 degrees."

Remove the strips from the marinade and skewer each strip straight through with one end of the strip hanging down. As many as seven strips can be placed on each skewer. Place the filled skewer in a hole on the jerky maker top. The strips should hang down and drip over the pan. Make sure the pieces do not touch each other and slow down the drying process.

With the oven turned down to 190 degrees, place the filled jerky maker in the oven. Be sure to use an oven thermometer to maintain the right temperature. (Do not use this jerky maker in a microwave oven.) The oven door should be kept closed unless it does not cycle below 200 degrees. In that case the oven door should be cracked open during the drying process. The drying time will vary depending on the thickness of the meat and the actual oven temperature. Use mitts to remove the hot metal jerky maker from the oven.

To take the jerky off of the skewers, first let it completely cool, then slide your thumb and index finger down the skewer. Jerky is dark brown when it's done, it's flexible and not brittle. Store jerky in an airtight container. This jerky maker is dishwasher safe.

21

MOTHER'S CAJUN MADNESS

4 tablespoons teriyaki sauce
3 tablespoons brown sugar
2 tablespoons spicy steak sauce
2 tablespoons cayenne pepper
1 tablespoon plain meat tenderizer
1 tablespoon cajun spice
1/4 teaspoon pineapple juice
1 dash crushed red pepper

2 pounds ground meat

Mix the ingredients, then add meat and let marinate for at least one hour, then dry.

MOTHER'S FAVORITE

5 tablespoons soy sauce
3 tablespoons liquid smoke
3 tablespoons water
3 tablespoons brown sugar
1 tablespoon black pepper
1/2 tablespoon plain meat tenderizer
1/4 teaspoon onion powder
1/4 teaspoon garlic powder

2 pounds ground meat

Mix the ingredients, then add meat and let marinate for at least one hour, then dry.

MOTHER'S HOT STUFF

5 tablespoons soy sauce
3 tablespoons liquid smoke
3 tablespoons brown sugar
3 tablespoons water
1 tablespoon black pepper
1 teaspoon cayenne pepper
1/2 tablespoon plain meat tenderizer
1/4 teaspoon onion powder
1/4 teaspoon garlic powder

2 pounds ground meat

Mix the ingredients, then add meat and let marinate for at least one hour, then dry.

MOTHER'S SOUTHERN TWIST

1 cup soy sauce
1/2 cup red wine
1/2 cup water
1/3 cup sugar
1/2 teaspoon onion powder
1/2 teaspoon garlic powder
1/2 teaspoon black pepper
1/2 teaspoon Tabasco® sauce
1/4 teaspoon salt

2 pounds ground meat

Mix the ingredients, then add meat and let marinate for at least one hour, then dry.

MOTHER'S MID-WEST STYLE

2/3 cup Worcestershire sauce
2/3 cup soy sauce
1 tablespoon salt
1 teaspoon black pepper
1 teaspoon garlic powder
1 teaspoon onion powder

Optional: 1 tablespoon liquid smoke

2 pounds ground meat

Mix the ingredients, then add meat and let marinate for at least one hour, then dry.

MOTHER'S TERIYAKI KICK

5 tablespoons teriyaki sauce
3 tablespoons brown sugar
3 tablespoons water
3 tablespoons liquid smoke
1 tablespoon black pepper
1/2 tablespoon plain meat tenderizer
1 teaspoon cayenne pepper
1/4 teaspoon garlic powder
1/4 teaspoon onion powder

2 pounds ground meat

Mix the ingredients, then add meat and let marinate for at least one hour, then dry.

BROOKLYN JERKY

Stacy

Ah, Brooklyn, heart of cattle country and birthplace of some great beef jerky.

Wait! Brooklyn? Heart of the cattle country? Is there a Brooklyn, Kansas? A Brooklyn, Colorado? A Brooklyn, Texas?

Nope.

We're talking Brooklyn, New York, home of "da best" jerky around, say a group of locals at a hangout affectionately known as "the Corner." This is because of the efforts of Stacy, a Brooklynite by way of Mount Diablo in northern California.

Stacy, you see, was a jerky child. She has jerky in her blood like native Brooklynites have Ma's pot roast or spaghetti and meatballs in theirs. Stacy grew up with a jerky-making hipster mother in the early, "make-wine-not-war" seventies. Her mom made jerky from a recipe she learned from a "hippie church friend," Stacy recalled.

"Making jerky was a family thing—my mom, my brother and I hung thin slices of marinated meat in an electric oven using paper clips. We propped open the door with a spoon," Stacy recalled. "Oh, the smell of jerky throughout the night! How I loved that smell!"

While at college, Stacy continued using the paper-clips-in-the-oven method. Then she moved to Brooklyn.

"Wow! Talk about culture shock!" she said. "So many places to eat!"

After putting on a little extra weight, she decided to go on the high-protein, low-calorie Atkins diet, which recommended jerky as a snack. This was not a problem for a jerky-blooded woman like Stacy, except she couldn't find any. To her shock, most Brooklynites had never even heard of jerky, let alone eaten it. She finally found a passable jerky in a local convenience store, but she had fonder memories of her family's homemade jerky.

That's when she pulled out her mother's recipe and started making her own. Then, when her new friends sampled it (most for the first time), they encouraged her to continue. Then a friend's parents bought her a five-tray food dehydrator so she could make more of it, faster and her jerky-making passion took a serious turn.

"At the Corner hangout, Vinny, Tony and Tina and just about everyone else loved it," Stacy said. "Now, it's almost out of hand! If I don't bring jerky with me they scream, 'Where's my jerky?'"

Powered by this kind of enthusiasm, Stacy set about trying to make the best, most perfect jerky. She experimented with different recipes and processes. She tried flank steak, London broil and brisket, before settling on bottom round roast, which she prefers because it's nicely marbled. She bought meat from a local butcher until a friend with connections hooked her up with a wholesaler.

Family, friends and denizens of the Corner finally settled on teriyaki and hickory-smoked jerky as her best. Stacy gladly shared the basic recipe below, although she chose not to specify amounts or name the salt seasoning because she's considering making jerky her business.

As her jerky became more popular, Stacey bought a 30-tray dehydrator and a vacuum packer. The new dehydrator is faster and less messy because it has special mesh sheets that make cleaning easier. "When I get all 30 trays on my dehydrator it practically reaches the ceiling," she said. "I can make three 5-pound roasts at one time using all 30 trays."

Stacy is investigating ways to turn her passion for jerky into a profitable business. Meanwhile, she spends weekends up to her ceiling in jerky, while gradually spreading the word around New York. It's still not cattle country, but, thanks to Stacy, it's gradually becoming jerky country.

BROOKLYN TERIYAKI JERKY

Freeze the roast whole, overnight, then let it thaw for about two hours the next day before slicing it. Stacy prefers a meat slicer to get the thinnest possible strips.

4 pound bottom round roast
Kikkoman's Teriyaki Sauce™
Onion powder
Garlic powder
Seasoning salt
Crushed red pepper flakes

Place the strips in a bowl and cover with the teriyaki, onion and garlic powder, then let it marinate.

"The longer you marinate, the stronger the flavor and the more tender the jerky. The marinade becomes a tenderizer," Stacy said.

Lay the strips on the dehydrator tray and sprinkle them with seasoning salt and crushed red pepper flakes before putting them in a 155-degree dehydrator.

GLENDA'S GREAT JERKIES

Glenda Ohs

I first met Glenda Ohs a few years ago when she stopped by my booth at the Minnesota State Fair to talk about making elk jerky. Originally from northern Minnesota, Glenda moved to the Tobacco Root Mountain foothills in southwestern Montana in 1968. "You'd love it out here," she said enthusiastically. "Right outside my front window is Hollow Top Mountain. At almost 11,000 feet it has snow on its peak year round. Once I counted 18 antelope, 88 mule deer and seven white tail deer within my yard".

"I've got a great pemmican recipe," she said enthusiastically. Traditionally, pemmican was pounded dried meat, fat and berry paste that was stuffed into airtight animal skins. It is a high protein, calorie-rich, concentrated snack food in a portable, compact form. The Native American people are credited for developing it and it became a mainstay as the west was settled.

"I like eating jerky and apple leather together," she chuckled. "So one day I scratched my head and thought, why not put the two together?"

GLENDA'S PEMMICAN

Glenda's pemmican involves three steps. First, she makes her Arizona cousin's favorite ground meat jerky, then she makes apple-sauce and then combines them. "You can use any kind of ground meat, but elk is the best."

STEP 1:
ARIZONA JERKY

6 tablespoons Worcestershire
    sauce
6 teaspoons soy sauce
2 teaspoons garlic powder
2 teaspoons onion powder
2 teaspoons salt
½ teaspoon jalapeno powder
½ teaspoon black pepper
½ teaspoon cinnamon

3 pounds lean ground elk

Mix all the ingredients together. You can use a jerky gun to make 5-inch long strips or spread the meat mixture onto a fruit leather sheet and cut it into strips later. Dry at a temperature of at least 145 degrees. The important thing to remember is to dry the jerky just to the point where it is still a little tacky. If the jerky is completely dry, the fruit sauce won't stick to it.

STEP 2:
APPLE LEATHER

Core apples and grind them in a blender, or buy a jar of natural, unsweetened applesauce. "I like crab apples because they're tart, but any apple or any kind of fruit will do," she said.

1 cup crab apple puree
1 tablespoon honey
½ teaspoon lemon juice

Puree ingredients until smooth.

STEP 3:
PEMMICAN

While the jerky is still tacky, spread a layer of applesauce on top of it about ⅛-inch thick. Return the coated jerky to the dehydrator, where it should dry in a couple of hours. Dry until the applesauce is no longer sticky. If you like, turn the pemmican over, coat the other side and dry again.

ELK JERKY

"My little ranch is very productive," she said. On 1,070 acres she raises alfalfa hay, barley, wheat, oats, canola as well as green pea seeds for the Jolly Green Giant. Over winter she pastures as many as 270 riding horses and each spring midwifes about 100 calving cows.

"Last fall one of the men shot an elk and a deer. After we butchered them, we removed the gristle and fat from the larger cuts and froze them. The important thing about big game is that the fat has to be completely trimmed off, because that's what carries the strong wild taste," she said. "I saved the poorer cuts for making ground meat jerky."

To make jerky Glenda pulls the semi-frozen chunks of meat into pieces about ¼-inch thick and 5 inches long. Her marinating process is simple: Put a layer of meat strips in a crock, sprinkle it with salt, pepper and a little liquid smoke, add another layer of meat, more salt, pepper, smoke, then a little teriyaki sauce. Repeat this process until the crock is full. Cover it with a pie plate, put a rock on top and let it sit in a cool room overnight. In the morning, remove the strips from the brine and dry them either in a dehydrator at 155 degrees or put them in an 180 degree oven, or air dry them.

OVEN-DRIED JERKY

"When I use the oven, I line the bottom with aluminum foil to catch any juice that drips down. I lay the strips on a cookie sheet in a single row or set them right on the oven rack. Don't let the strips touch or overlap each other, because you need as much dry air as possible to get to all the surfaces of the drying meat.

"When I use a cookie sheet I turn the pieces over at least once so the bottom can get dry. When I put the strips on an oven rack, I first spray the rack with an aerosol oil. This makes it easier to get the jerky off. When the jerky is dry, I let it cool, then put it in plastic bags and store in my freezer."

AIR-DRIED JERKY

On hot, dry days, after brining the meat overnight, Glenda lays the strips on wax paper and places them all over her house. "They're on the counter, on the table, on top of the microwave, on my desk, they are on every flat surface," she laughed. During this two-day drying event, the dogs and cats have to stay out of the house. On day two she turns all the slices over. "I like to air dry jerky because it doesn't have a cooked taste," she said.

GLENDA'S STRIP JERKY

Morton's™ and Moore's Old Farm Meat Cure™, two of her favorite flavorings are available in most grocery stores. Glenda also uses these cures to make jerky, bacon, pepperoni and pastrami.

9 teaspoons either Morton's or Moore's Old Farm Meat Cure
3 teaspoons Accent™
2 teaspoons black pepper
2 teaspoons garlic powder
1½ teaspoons Morton Tender Quick™
1 teaspoon ground cardamom
1 teaspoon red cayenne pepper
1 teaspoon liquid smoke
3 pounds elk strips

Mix the ingredients together, then add meat strips. Let marinate overnight. Then lay strips in a drying environment.

SMOKED WHITEFISH

Glenda made the following brine when her neighbor went ice fishing on the Jefferson River and brought her 30 whitefish. Whitefish have a high fat content, so she made a strong brine.

"I like using sweet woods, like cherry and apple. It took me about 10 hours to smoke the 30 fish," she said.

GLENDA'S BRINE

1 gallon water
1 cup non-iodized salt
½ cup brown sugar
2 tablespoons lemon concentrate
1 teaspoon garlic powder
⅛ tablespoon onion powder

30 whitefish filets

Combine the ingredients and stir until dissolved. Add fish filets and soak overnight. Rinse. Let the fish strips air-dry at least two hours. "It's really important to let them dry a little, because it makes a far superior dried product," she advised. She dried them in her electric smoker set at 185 degrees.

Glenda's raw whitefish.

NATIVE AMERICAN JERKY

Larry Belitz

Larry Belitz and I share a love of the same book, *Buffalo Bird Woman's Garden.* This book is a record of Buffalo Bird Woman's own words. It tells the truth about what life was like being a Hidatsa woman in a village called Like-a-fishhook on the Missouri River in North Dakota in the 1800s. In my opinion it is a work of art. It details how food was grown, cared for, harvested, preserved and used.

Larry first became interested in the Lakota Sioux people because of his uncle who was an agent, working with them. Larry was drawn to their self-sufficient ways and how they lived with and off of the land.

"Everything revolved around the buffalo," he said. "They provided the first Americans with food, clothing and a way of life. Horns were shaped into utensils. Ribs were made into sled runners. Hides became ropes, shields, bull boats, parfleches and teepees. Meat became jerky.

"To make jerky they isolated each muscle. Using a knife that was beveled only on one side, they cut along the entire length of the muscle with the grain, then pulled off the surrounding thin membranes. This is different from the way white men cut meat across grain to make their jerky."

The preferred muscle was the tenderloin. One purpose of this cutting method was to end

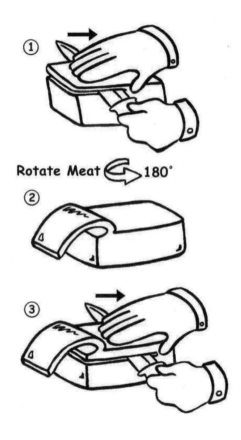

Rotate Meat ⟲ 180°

up with one long continuous strip of meat, like an accordion pleat. When unfolded it could be as long as two feet.

To do this the muscle must be laid flat so that it is easy to cut. With one hand placed firmly on top of the meat, and following the grain, slicing is begun at one end, parallel to the work surface and $1/8$-inch below the top. Working across the meat, the knife is stopped $1/8$-inch short of the other end. The slab of meat is not cut all the way through. The goal is to make the next cut so that a hinge that bends is created.

The knife is removed and the meat is turned around 180 degrees. A second cut is begun at $1/8$-inch deep. One hand is firmly planted on the newly exposed top. The cutting across is continued and again stopped $1/8$-inch from the end. The meat is turned and cut until the last piece is $1/8$-inch thick. Then it is unfolded, stretched and laid over drying poles. A stick is laid across the meat so when the wind blows hard it would keep the meat strips from sticking together.

The Lakota call dried meat—deer, antelope, buffalo—"bapa." Absolutely no flavorings, including salt are used. "Two myths that need to be changed are that Native Americans used smoke to help dry their food. (That happened only when it rained.) Second, salt was not a common commodity." Larry explained that meat dried without salt holds up better because salt is hydroscopic, meaning it picks water up from the air. This was a serious disadvantage when airtight storage space was not available.

"Sometimes when the dry South Dakota wind was strong, the meat strips would dry in as little as two hours, rarely did it take more than one day to make jerky."

To the Native American, jerky has been a prominent cooking ingredient. They added jerky to their dried bean, dried corn and dried turnip soups. To dry prairie turnips, they dug the root, cut the flowering part off, peeled the roots and braided these little bulbs together. It looked like a garlic string. If they were not peeled they would turn black, the braid was hung in the sun to dry. Turnips were rehydrated in water along with dried buffalo. Turnips provided the starch and tasted like potatoes. When corn was in the milk stage it was boiled, then dried. To dry pumpkins, they peeled off rind in such a way to make one continuous spiral.

Although Larry is not a native American, he was adopted into the Lakota tribe because of his passion for native ways and his dedication to practicing them. "At first I learned to do porcupine quill work. Porcupine quills were used for decoration long before beads. Beads came with Lewis and Clark. I am a purist and enjoy being meticulous," he said. "My wife and I travel all over the country to museums. We draw what catches our interest. We feel we learn more by drawing instead of taking photos."

His fascination of the Native American way has dominated his life. He has constructed 33 bison hide teepees just as Plains Indians did, he gives workshops on tanning, quill work, flint knapping and he has been involved in several documentaries. He was a technical advisor for the movie Dances With Wolves and he wrote *Brain Tanning the Sioux Way.* Larry also runs a museum mail order business that offers Plains Indian items that were made before 1870.

PEMMICAN

"Wasna," Sioux for pemmican, was made by pounding bapa. If ever a time came that I had to rely on my own devices to continue to live I would make a ton of pemmican. When hungry, I'd take a pinch, stick it in my mouth and enjoy a high protein, high energy lunch.

Native Americans pounded dried chokecherries or June berries and added it to the pounded jerky. Melted fat was poured over the mixture to keep it together and to form patties. Kidney fat was preferred because it didn't turn rancid. Any of the following dried foods can be added to pemmican: a handful of dried rose hips will provide vitamin C; or add any dried wild fruit such as plums, strawberries, grapes, raspberries, cherries, huckleberries, or service berry or buffalo berries or blueberries.

MY FAVORITE PEMMICAN
1½ cups jerky
1 cup peanut butter
½ cup dried blueberries
½ cup dried chopped apricots
½ cup raisins or apples or wild plums, buffalo berries or acid berry

Grind the jerky in a blender into a coarse powder. Combine all ingredients and shape into 18 one-inch balls or sticks.

38

A TRICKY STICK

Manny Howard

My telephone rang. "Have you read the article in the Food section of The New York Times Magazine about reverse engineering a Slim Jim? Ira Newman asked.

"No," I replied.

One week later a copy of the article arrived. I telephoned Ira. "It's perfect," I said.

"Include it," Ira demanded.

Luckily the New York Times gave permission to reprint it.

The Slim Jim was created by Adolph Levis in Philadelphia in the 1940's. After an unsuccessful early career as a violinist and a failed effort to operate a string of tobacco shops, Levis and a partner had turned to the pickled-food trade, hawking pig's feet, cabbage and cucumbers to bars and taverns in and around Philadelphia. Pepperoni, he noticed, was becoming popular among his clientele, and he made an end run around the fad by creating a preserved meat product that, rather than curing for weeks, could be manufactured in a matter of days by a process of fermentation and hot smoking

The snack sold well in the bars, first in Philadelphia and then up and down the East Coast. Eventually, a bidding war broke out over Slim Jim's name and recipe, and in 1967, Levis (pronounced LEV-iss) and his partner sold out to General Mills, for $20 million. The brand would pass through three other companies in the ensuing years, and each time it did, the recipe changed a little, to make production cheaper and more efficient. They even started putting chicken into the original all-beef formula. What at first required just 10 common ingredients now calls for 31. But the taste, everyone agrees, remains true to Levis's original.

The sale of anything, even a stick of dried meat, to a company like General Mills pretty much assures that the instructions for making it become an industrial secret. So when we decided to make a Levis-era Slim Jim, as a salute to its inventor who died this year, we got no help from its current owner, ConAgra. They wished us luck and sent us on our way.

Undeterred, we went to Harvey Brodsky, Levis's son-in-law, who told us he didn't know the original recipe. "It's not like we've got it written down in family scrapbooks," he said good-naturedly. He supplied one critical clue, however: the use of lactic acid is crucial in the fermentation process because it lowers the pH and imparts a unique tanginess.

We realized that we would have to go freelance, and so our next stop was Wade Moises, the sous-chef and butcher at Lupa restaurant in New York. He is that rare breed, a sausage geek, and he was certain that he could help us reverse-engineer a Slim Jim. Though he did have some reservations. Before settling down to work, he snapped off a piece of a Slim Jim, chewed it and winced. "You sure you want to do this?"

From Bruce Aidells, the man who restored the good name of mass-produced sausage in America, we learned that Levis's original recipe was probably based on an Eastern European thin rope sausage, usually made with pork and beef, because "its spices are mild and it takes the smoke well."

A recipe for rope sausage, provided by Aidells, has ten ingredients (not counting the meat and the fat), like the original Slim Jim. The heat comes from white and black pepper; Moises suggested using cayenne instead and doubling the salt. "The meat-to-fat ratio is very important and so is the amount of lactic acid," he says, dropping pieces of top-round chuck and beef fat into a meat grinder. "After that, it's a question of adjusting the spices."

Making sausage is really quite straightforward. The meat is ground, then kneaded together with spices, lactic-acid starter (freeze-dried milk, essentially) and a pink curing salt. The meat-and-spice mixture has to be kneaded until it is doughy and can be squeezed through the sausage press and into the sheathing. Slim Jims are now cased in collagen, but we figure that the originals were natural. So we go with lamb intestines, which are properly narrow.

A sausage maker close to the Slim Jim production process, speaking on the condition of anonymity, revealed to us that a Slim Jim is smoked at between 110 and 140 degrees for 22 hours and then allowed to cool at 50 degrees with next to no humidity. So that's what we do.

After tasting the first batch, we decide it needs an additional two tablespoons of salt and eight more ounces of fat to make it into Slim Jim territory. By the third generation, we think we have something close, so we let it dry overnight in a refrigerator and then smoke it. "I think we got it," says Moises, looking up from his prep work on the fifth day of our project. "It could be a bit greasier, but the spice and the tanginess is there."

41

We send a package of our homemade Slim Jims overnight to Brodsky. He is defensive and not at all complimentary. "The samples are way off," he says in a voice-mail message. "The color is wrong, the chop is wrong, the consistency of the casing is wrong. The spicing just doesn't seem to be there, and the lactic-acid starter culture? Didn't taste any."

We decide not to take his word for it, and as his father-in-law might have done, we head out to a local tavern. At Montero's, hard by the Brooklyn docks, a regular sits at the bar. "You made your own Slim Jim?" he says, as if he has heard this one already too. When I ask if he'd try one and tell me if it tastes like the Slim Jims of old, he wrinkles up his face and says, "Why not?"

He chews for a moment, then shrugs. "Sure," he says. "You made a Slim Jim. Good for you."

WADE MOISES'S TAKE ON THE ORIGINAL SLIM JIM
(ADAPTED FROM BRUCE AIDELLS)

1 lamb intestine casing (4 feet
 long)
½ pounds top round chuck, cubed
1 pound beef fat, cubed
3 tablespoons paprika
2 teaspoons black pepper
2 teaspoons cayenne pepper
½ teaspoon ground coriander
1 teaspoon ground fennel seeds
1 teaspoon No. 1 curing salt
2 teaspoons sugar
1 clove garlic, peeled and
 smashed
⅓ cup lactic-acid starter culture.

Rinse salt off the sausage casing.
Soak in ice water for at least 1 hour.

Combine meat and fat. Run the mixture through a meat grinder into a large bowl, using the finest setting. Add all ingredients, along with one cup of ice water. Knead vigorously until mixture is the consistency of bread dough (about 8 minutes).

Rinse casing one last time. Choose the narrowest gauge tube of your sausage press. Splash the tube with ice water, then pull the casing over it. Transfer the mixture, about two fistfuls at a time, to the sausage press and then pump the meat into the casing, splashing more water on the tubing as needed to stop the casing from tearing.

Preheat an electric smoker to 100 degrees. Hang sausage in the smoker for 22 hours. The temperature should never dip below 90 degrees or go above 110 degrees. After 22 hours, raise the temperature to 150 degrees and cook until the internal temperature reaches 150 to 155 degrees (about 30 minutes).

Remove from smoker and let cool at about 50 degrees in a dry place for 4 hours. Cut sausage into 4-inch lengths. Yield: 16 servings.

A PROVEN JERKY THEORY

Dr. Larry Borchert

After retiring as Director of Research from the Oscar Mayer Food Corporation, Dr. Larry Borchert became an adjunct professor in the Meat Science Department at the University of Wisconsin in Madison.

While doing his post-doctoral work in Germany, he developed a theory based on his study of a type of pork that gave up its water really easily. "This pork rapidly went down to an isoelectric point of pH 5.3, which meant it quickly reached its lowest water holding capacity. I speculated that if this type of pork was used as an ingredient in salami it would dry faster," he said.

"I now know that the way to accomplish this reaction in other meats is to add an organic acid such as vinegar or lemon juice."

Larry has been a hunter since the age of 14, so his profession and hobby work well together. "I've always handled venison and have experimented with ways to make jerky since the mid-1970s," he said.

We get the benefit of both his profession and hobby in the following jerky formula, which uses natural food acids to help meat reach its lowest water-holding capacity. The formula was first published in 1998 by the United States Department of Agriculture Project, with the aim of developing products for under-utilized red meat species, such as wild game, or bison, ostrich and emu.

45

"Each ingredient plays an essential role," Larry explained. "Sodium nitrite is always included because without it meat loses its fresh flavor and natural color. Nitrite also retards the growth of microbial pathogens. The action of salt without nitrite is to oxidize and, in time, turn the meat rancid. Soy sauce contributes more salt and moves the pH in the right direction. Worcestershire sauce is the key ingredient because it is about 65 percent vinegar, which has a drying effect."

TIP: A less expensive substitute for Worcestershire sauce is a mixture of 60 percent vinegar and 40 percent soy sauce.

PER 100 POUNDS

For venison, elk and bison, Larry says to use lean flank or round muscles. For ostrich and emu, use denuded (desilvered) cuts such as the round, tip, strip, oyster or drum. Trim off all visible fat and connective tissue.

4 pounds salt
4 ounces sodium nitrite
  (6.25 percent nitrite pre-mix)
8 ounces ground black pepper
8 ounces garlic powder
8 ounces onion powder
5.5 pounds soy sauce
6.8 pounds Worcestershire sauce

"Prior to marinating, freeze the whole muscle, then bring it back to a high sub-freezing temperature. It should be still firm enough to make nice $1/8$ to $1/4$-inch slices along the muscle fiber grain. Freezing physically damages the cells enough so they give up their moisture more readily. Although freezing is usually hard on meat it has great benefit when making jerky."

The way Larry explains it, marinating is a three-fold process.

"First, I evenly apply dry ingredients to the semi-frozen meat slices. As the meat thaws, the ingredients become absorbed. I leave it for 24 hours at 40 degrees. The second day, I do what I call an overhaul. I start at the top taking each piece of meat and putting it on bottom of another pan. At the same time I put soy sauce on each piece. The meat slices soak up the sauce like a sponge. Then I let it cure again at 40 degrees for another 24 hours. The third day I bring on the Worcestershire sauce, which has the opposite effect of causing the proteins to give up moisture. By the fourth day every bit of moisture has been sucked up into the meat. There is no brine."

He places the meat on racks, leaving space in between the strips so the air can circulate. He dries them until the jerky is firm and dry to the touch. To retain high quality, Larry advises vacuum-packing.

"I'm not advocating this, but I never use heat to dry meat. I dry it at a cool temperature, with or without forced air. In the lab I dry it below 60 degrees using forced air and it dries in 18 to 24 hours. It comes out dry, yet flexible, with a mahogany color and a good natural meat flavor."

I must add a note of caution here, Larry is able to make jerky at such a low temperature because of the addition of sodium nitrite, without it there could be a bacterial risk.

JERKED CHICKEN JERKY

Evan Clark

I love being a writer, especially when a story calls me! In this case, Evan Clark sent an e-mail asking me about taking jerky backpacking.

"I got your dehydrator cookbook for Christmas," he began. "Now I'm off on a 4^1/$_2$ month hike on the Appalachian Trail with my soon-to-be wife and I need to know how to store jerky so it can be sent in food drop boxes and still be edible in the latter stages of our hike. Any suggestions?"

This was my reply to Evan's question: "After your jerky has cooled and you've made sure its thoroughly dry, either vacuum pack it or put it in heavy plastic bags and store it in your freezer. Then just before your trip, take it out, check to make sure that no ice crystals have formed inside the package and send it ahead."

As we exchanged e-mails, Evan's story became more interesting when I learned that he'd met the woman destined to become his wife two years earlier while walking the Appalachian Trail. She was heading north. He was heading south. They exchanged business cards, corresponded and are getting married just before starting their Appalachian adventure together.

"I love the Appalachian Trail," Evan said. "I started backpacking to celebrate my 40th birthday. I carried 63 pounds on my back. It was torture. I had to make deals with myself. I'd walk

49

40 steps and only then could I stoop over and rest. I seldom took my backpack off because it was too painful to hoist on my back."

Leaving Mt. Katahdin, Maine, to begin their hike, Evan and his fiancée each will carry 30-pound packs with enough food for one week. At two pounds a day, they'll have nuts for calories; corn pasta (which provides more energy than wheat pasta); orange-juice-soaked banana chips (another creative use of a food dehydrator); and lots of jerked chicken jerky for protein. Every week they'll pick up a food drop package until they reach Springer Mountain, Georgia, in mid-October.

Evan invented his recipe for Jerked Chicken Jerky after returning from working as a Peace Corps Volunteer in Jamaica—the island of wonderful food and exotic tastes. He loved the spicy/hot flavor of jerked chicken so much, and wanted to be able to take it along on his backpacking trips, so he bought a dehydrator and experimented until he got his chicken jerk just right.

TIP: Cooking helps destroy bacteria and improves the storing quality. Dried, raw poultry can become hard and tasteless, whereas cooked, dried chicken tastes better and reconstitutes faster.

JERKED CHICKEN JERKY

One of the main ingredients is Walkerswood Traditional Jamaican Jerk Seasoning™, which Evan found in a Mexican grocery store in Washington, D.C. The seasoning includes scallions, scotch bonnet peppers, salt, black pepper, allspice, nutmeg, citric acid, sugar and thyme.

"Be careful with that stuff," he warned. "It's extremely hot." The scotch bonnet peppers that make the jerk burn grow on pepper trees in the Caribbean. The people who process them must wear rubber gloves to protect their skin."

50

1 tablespoon olive oil
2 teaspoons Traditional Jamaican
   Jerk Seasoning
1 teaspoon salt
2 fresh limes

1 pound boneless, skinless
   chicken breasts

Put oil, jerk spice, salt and squeeze the lime juice into a sealable plastic bag. Cut partially frozen chicken in to 1/4-inch thick slices that are 1/2-inch wide and up to 5 inches long. Put them into the bag, seal and shake thoroughly so all the strips receive the benefit of the marinade. Place the bag in the refrigerator 24 to 36 hours. During this time the acid in the lime juice almost cooks as well as tenderizes the chicken. Pre-heat the oven to 300 degrees. Lay the strips in a single layer on a cookie sheet and bake 30 minutes. Let the chicken strips cool, then lay them on a dehydrator tray and dry at 145 degrees for 8 to 12 hours.

JERKING THE BLUE GOOSE

Bob Follmer

Bob Follmer loves to hunt, to cook and to eat. The day his doctor told him he had congestive heart failure and had to limit his salt intake, which meant he had to stop eating sausage and jerky, Bob decided it was time to take control. "I bought a dehydrator and started making my own salt-free jerky. The salt-laden store stuff was history," Bob said. "They add salt because it's a cheap way to add flavor. Drinking establishments sell salty stuff because it encourages customers to drink."

After making his first batch of goose jerky, Bob took four pounds of it with him on a trip to Grandville, North Dakota with his hunting buddies. During the 8-hour drive they devoured it all. "Since that trip they expect jerky every time we get together," he chuckled. "We hunt Blue and Snow geese. They're greasier birds than the honker and I've tried every which way to eat them. So it was out of necessity that I started using them to make jerky."

Bob handed me a sample of his jerky. It tasted sweet and tart at the same time.

"My goose marinade works for any meat," he said. "I've used it for venison, turkey, beef and anything else I can get my hands on. It has more flavor than any recipe I've tried." Bob has methodically kept a journal of his jerky-making experiments since 1979.

After skinning the bird, he

uses only the breast and thigh for the jerky, leaving the legs behind because they are too bony, and he trims off all the fat. "You've got to trim off all the fat or the jerky will taste rancid," he cautioned. He cuts the raw, purplish goose meat in strips about $1/4$-inch thick and one inch wide.

Although Bob has made goose jerky in his electric smoker and in the oven, he prefers using a dehydrator because it makes sampling easier. "The smell of goose jerky drying drives me nuts," he confessed. "I can't wait until it's ready. I keep opening up the lid and sampling it."

Bob says it takes just as long to use an electric oven. When he uses the oven he props open the door open with a folded potholder to allow moist air to escape.

GOOSE JERKY MARINADE

"When I make this for my wife I eliminate the Tabasco sauce and pepper because she doesn't like it hot. However, for my buddies who do like it hot, I kick it up a notch by adding 3 tablespoons of habanero pepper powder."

When I asked how he stored his jerky, he replied with a grin, "My jerky never makes it that far. If my family doesn't get it, the neighbors do."

I can beer
1 cup cheap red cooking wine
3/4 cup light soy sauce
3/4 cup Worcestershire sauce
1/2 cup Kikkoman teriyaki sauce
1/2 cup lemon juice
1/3 cup liquid smoke
3 tablespoons onion powder
3 tablespoons garlic powder
3 tablespoons Accent seasoning
2 tablespoons Tabasco sauce
2 tablespoons Caribbean jerk
    seasoning
1 tablespoon black pepper

4 pounds goose strips

Put all the marinade ingredients in
a large plastic bowl, blend, then
add the strips. Cover the bowl and
put it in the refrigerator. Turn the
meat every 12 hours, so everything gets well soaked. Marinate
48 to 96 hours.

He dries the strips in a dehydrator
at 155 degrees. After about
10 hours his jerky is soft, easy
to chew and good-tasting, which
is how he likes it. "I leave some
in 14 hours for my sons because
they like it dried hard as a rock
and then it turns almost black."

JERKY CANDY

Billy Hagberg

"Candy"—that's what Billy Hagberg calls his beef, chicken and turkey jerky.

"At our meat counter we hand out jerky samples. People come in, stand in front of the counter, they try a piece of this and a little of that. Pretty soon they're acting like kids pondering which piece of 'candy' they want next," Billy said, flashing a warm and friendly smile.

Billy is in charge of making the jerky at the Hagberg Country Market in Lake Elmo, Minnesota. This family market has provided meat, poultry and fish to Minnesota and Wisconsin customers since the 1938 Depression.

"My great grandparents brought an old family holiday sausage recipe with them when they came here from Sweden," Billy recalled. "That's really how our business got started. They used a lot of different meats in those days. Me, I prefer jerky made from top round beef, or with chicken or turkey breasts."

Billy uses a vacuum tumbler to process the raw meat. It is an excellent technique because the result is a moist, tender, easy-to-chew jerky that has a uniform texture, an outstanding aroma and a rich color.

"Getting that vacuum drum was the best decision we ever made," Billy said. "Before we got the vacuum unit we had to soak our meat strips in a marinade or a brine for 24 to 48 hours. That means using a lot of containers, as well as taking up too much floor and refrigerator space. Now, with the vacuum drum, we marinate strips for about 20 minutes," Billy boasted. "When space matters, this is an answer. Now we don't have containers sitting everywhere around our shop."

Salt is generally the main brine ingredient. One major disadvantage of a long brining time is that salt leeches blood out of meat, but blood is a flavoring agent and dried meat has less flavor without it.

Using the vacuum tumbler allows Billy to use less brine, less salt and, "we don't have to use any fancy, expensive ingredients because the jerky has more natur-

al flavor," he explained.

What is this vacuum tumbler, anyway? Basically, it's a 20-gallon stainless steel cylinder drum with an opening on one side and a removable lid. The drum Billy uses can hold 35 to 50 pounds of strips at one time. You fill the drum, secure the lid, flick a switch and the drum rotates. As it rotates, it agitates and tenderizes the meat. The vacuum pump draws the air out of the chamber, which creates a negative pressure so the meat pores open up, spread apart and the flavorings are forced deep into the tissues. It takes Billy only 20 minutes to complete the vacuum-tumbling process.

"You get three to four times higher concentration of flavor, in

Daniel's Food Equipment 50 pound capacity vaccum tumbler.

comparison to the long-term brining," Billy said.

After you get good at it, you can adjust the amount of marinade or brine to the weight of the strips, so there is 100 percent absorption and zero waste.

"All the marinade goes inside the meat," Billy said. "Doesn't that make more sense than throwing the marinade down the drain? Plus, we get a more consistent product. Since the processing time is dramatically reduced, there is less risk of contamination and that's critical when meeting food inspection standards."

After tumbling the strips, Billy lets them "rest" in the refrigerator overnight. In the morning he spreads them on smoker trays and uses a mixture of maple and hickory wood for smoke. Because the strips are quite dry when they go into the smoker, that process is also faster. Once dry, the jerky is ready for his counter or vacuum packed and shipped.

"It's a good process for making small batches of jerky," Billy said.

LUTEFISK— JERKY BY ANOTHER NAME

"Ever hear of Lutefisk?" Billy asked, but before I could issue a full grunt, he continued, "It was the first reconstituted jerky I ever heard of."

Traditionally, cod was air-dried. Fishermen removed the head and split the cod (or a similar fish with a low-fat content) into two sides. They removed the backbone and cut the sides in long, narrow strips about an inch wide. The fish, still joined together by the collarbone, was washed thoroughly, salted and hung outside in the dry North Atlantic air for up to a week, depending upon the weather and the size of the fish.

According to Billy, Scandinavian fishing ships carried dried cod with them. When they wanted a good meal they'd reconstitute the fish in lye until it reached a gelatinous consistency, then they'd wash it well and have a feast.

"If you want to try it," Billy said, daring me with a smile, "buy a jar of lutefisk, the stuff that's already soaking, wash it in cold water, soak it overnight in clean water, then drain it and put it in a glass or enamel pan (not aluminum), add water and salt. Cover it with aluminum foil and bake it at 400 degrees for 20 minutes. Pour melted butter over it and serve with boiled potatoes and lefse."

As he finished his instructions, I remembered something someone else once told me, about lutefisk being a miracle food—that just a few servings can feed a very large crowd.

MIKE'S WILD CATFISH JERKY

Mike Valley

Fishing is in Mike Valley's blood. As a boy he fished the Mississippi River with his father, just as all the men in his family did since the mid-1800s. He was 14 when he launched his own boat to run gill nets for buffalo and sheephead carp.

Every morning from April through October, before the sun rises, Mike, a strong, muscled man, steps into his 24-foot aluminum boat, starts the 230-horse Johnson engine and does what he loves most—he gets out on the Mississippi River.

"My favorite time is when the water is high," he said, with a boyish Huck Finn glint in his eye. "There have been times the water was so high that when I raised my nets there were a thousand pounds of fish."

"Sometimes I weave my boat in and out of the trees. I'll cut my engine, then sit and watch the waves lap up on the shore. I can't help but smile when I see a beaver resting on top of its house," he recalled as we visited in his shop overlooking the great Mississippi in Prairie du Chien, Wisconsin. "I love that river. Everything else is work. Time on the river is my payoff."

Mike has run into a lot of odd creatures in his years on the Mississippi. But he's most fascinated with the wild catfish.

"They're spooky," he said. "You can be looking at your fishfinder, thinking there's a solid object right underneath you, but it isn't, it's about a hundred cat-fish tightly bound together in an underwater community." Mike said. "If I'd drop something it would spook them and they'd explode in as many different directions as there were fish in the cluster."

"It's too bad the mud-cat got such a lousy name. In my opinion, it is a much better-tasting fish than a channel cat. The worse something smells, the more likely it is the channel-cat will bite on it—that should give you an indication of what it eats," he chuckled. "The mud-catfish is the one I use for jerky—it eats only live bait."

Mike explained more differences between the two fish. "A channel-cat has a tail fin that's deeply notched, while the mud-cat has a squarer tail that's only slightly notched. The mud-cat's head is flatter, it has heavy jaws and its lower mandible is longer than the upper. Some people call the mud-cat a flathead. The color differences change with age and environment."

Mike has a lot to say about fish, mud-cats in particular. "Mud-cats are nest builders. They are fascinating creatures. When spawning, the parents look out for the young until they are able to disperse. The young go to school as our kids do—or they stay in schools," he laughed. "Then when they are a little older, school is out and they go their own ways."

"The first year they reach about six inches in length. Adults on the Mississippi can reach over twenty inches and some grow to thirty or more pounds. There are fishing claims of catching 50 pound catfish between Clinton, Iowa, and Prairie du Chien, Wisconsin!"

In the early 1980s Mike started to develop his catfish jerky. "It took me years to get my jerky right," he said. "Everybody else was making jerky out of ground carp, but I wanted to use a boneless fish. I like the mud-cat because it has less oil than the channel-cat, so it doesn't burn as easily during the hot smoke-drying process. I suppose I could use pond-raised fish," his eyes darted toward the Mississippi, "but I like the wild catfish."

Mike and his wife, Lisa, filet the catfish, make their own brine, dry the fish in their smokehouse and sell the jerky in their shop. The process begins with cleaning about 500 pounds of fresh catfish, each fish weighing from four to 20 pounds. The head is cut off, it's gutted, then using only the belly pads, he filets each fish. This process generally takes Mike about six hours.

"The most important thing after the fish are filleted is to spray them with cold water, let them drain and not to wash them again," Mike instructed.

He lifted the top off a blue, 30-gallon plastic container,

reached in and got a handful of fish strips he'd prepared the day before. "I cut filets $1/4$-inch thick, $1/2$-inch wide and five or six inches long. Then I use a hot brine as a cure," he said. Looking a bit stern, he announced, "And I'm keeping my brine recipe secret. Basically you can use any jerky brine," he said. Then offered a word of advice: "Just be careful when adding salt. Too much salt can ruin any jerky."

After he's made his brine, he brings it to a boil for one minute, then simmers it for 10 minutes and lets it cool before putting the fish strips in to cure for about 15 hours.

Picking up the blue container, Mike walked from the pro-

Mike Valley placing marinated catfish on his smoker.

cessing room to a screened-in porch behind the shop that smelled intensely of smoke and fish. Dominating the space was a huge, black metal box standing about seven feet high, eight feet long and four feet deep. This blackened smoker had six enormous drawer-like trays.

Mike pulled out one tray, grabbed a steel brush and scraped the blackened steel. Mike's rough, weathered hands revealed a life of hard work. With the trays clean, he pulled open the bottom tray and spread out a handful of marinated catfish strips. It took him two hours to fill all six trays, carefully positioning each fish strip flat down. Almost whimsically he sprinkled a mixture of finely ground pepper, sweet basil and leaf oregano over the fish strips.

Walking around to the back of the smoker, he picked up a large cup and scooped a combination of two pounds of oak and hickory wood chips into a paper bag. Squatting down he opened the fire door, stuffed the bag in, laid two sticks on top and struck a match. The fire caught quickly and he shut the door. "I like using a mixture of chips." The teacher in him reappeared, "Never use pine or cedar because they can make jerky turn black."

He put a hand on his back to help himself up, then said, "I don't use wood that's been sprayed. It's got to be clean, without dirt, mold and not wormy."

"We burn about six truckloads of split hickory a year," he said, adding more wood. "I like using a little green hickory because it produces good smoke."

He glanced at the smokehouse thermometer, "It has to hit 160 degrees and stay there for at least 30 minutes during the smoking process. I've got to keep my eye on it. A whole batch can burn in just a few minutes." He stepped back. "A batch usually takes about four hours. You can tell when it's done because the fish jerky turns a beautiful golden color."

"The Wisconsin inspector said my smoke shop was the

cleanest in the state," Mike boasted as his wife Lisa, a friendly and attractive brunette, handed me my first sample of wild catfish jerky.

"That's wonderful," I said. "It smells stronger than it tastes."

"The quality standards we insist upon must be working," he said, "because we keep running out of our catfish jerky."

Their Valley Fish Shop is right off Wisconsin Highway 18, near the Wisconsin-Iowa bridge in Prairie du Chien, Wisconsin. If you're in the area, stop in for a sample of wild catfish jerky, and check out Mike's hand-carved decoys and signs—he's an artist as well as a jerky maker. Mike also has a video on cleaning, smoking and making fish jerky.

JUDY'S HAM JERKY

Judy Lynch

Judy Lynch and her husband Dan have worked with horses for over 30 years on a farm outside Madison, Wisconsin. Judy specializes in arranging and conducting pack trips throughout North America. Several years ago after leading a trip to the Bob Marshall Wilderness in Montana with 11 people and 18 horses, Judy returned feeling defeated. "I didn't know if I'd ever be able to go on another pack trip unless somehow it got easier," she recalled.

"Food preparation is the hardest part of a pack trip," she said. "My main job is to provide delicious, hearty meals. I love to cook and I take pride in serving good food. I want everyone to sit around our campfire, smack their lips and say, 'WOW! That was an incredible meal! How did you do that?'"

The trip to Montana haunted Judy until I (yes, me, Mary Bell) went to her farm looking to rekindle my relationship with horses. As Judy and I got to know each other, I invited her to a food drying class. I saw the light bulb turn on in her head as she tasted the dried food samples.

The next summer Judy returned to the Bob Marshall for a five-day pack trip with another large group. This time she had dehydrated all of the main meals. As a result, all of her kitchen and food supplies fit in one large duffel bag.

"Drying food and planning ahead was the key," she said hap-

67

pily. "I experienced less stress, my food budget was reduced, the horses packed lighter loads and everyone loved the food, including my husband, who enjoys traditional home cooking. He said it was the best trail food he'd ever eaten."

"Ham jerky was my biggest hit. Everybody loved it," she said. "Riders always want something salty to snack on and the ham jerky satisfied that desire— after all, bringing chips on a pack trip is not an easy task! It's a real good idea to have something salty to eat, because it makes the riders drink more water, which most of the time they don't do enough."

"I also liked that it was different," Judy said. "Most jerky is just dried red meat. I've made chicken jerky and we liked it as a snack, but I didn't like the way it rehydrated when I tried to use it as an ingredient in cooking. It seemed too tough, whereas the ham jerky rehydrated great and added zing and variety to my menu. A little ham jerky and a box of scalloped potatoes makes a dynamite meal."

Judy makes ham jerky from both ground ham and from strips. "I had my butcher grind a ham. I like snacking on ground ham jerky," she said.

GROUND HAM JERKY

1 pound ground ham
1 tablespoon Poupon™ mustard
1 tablespoon honey

Mix together, let marinate for 15 minutes, then shape into 1-inch thick strips that are 5 inches long. Dry at 145 degrees.

STRIP HAM JERKY

Judy simply cuts leftover honey-glazed ham in slices about ¼-inch thick, ½-inch wide and several inches long. She dries the slices in her dehydrator at 145 degrees for 6 hours. For ham jerky to be used as a cooking ingredient she cuts the ham into ¼- to ½-inch squares.

HAM CURRY WITH NOODLES

Judy says this "Wow!" meal will feed six hungry horseback riders.

4 cups ½-inch dehydrated ham squares
2 teaspoons dehydrated minced onions
6 tablespoons butter
6 tablespoons flour
2 teaspoons curry powder
¼ teaspoon pepper
½ teaspoon salt
2 chicken bouillon cubes
2 cups Milk Maid™ powdered milk
8 ounces medium noodles
1 cup dry Parmesan Cheese

To Package

Assemble five plastic bags and one plastic container. Place the following in each bag:

Bag 1: dehydrated ham and dehydrated onion
Bag 2: flour, curry powder, pepper, salt and chicken bouillon
Bag 3: powdered milk
Bag 4: noodles and salt
Bag 5: cheese

Put the butter in a plastic container that has a tight seal.

Place all five bags and the butter container in one 2-gallon sealable plastic bag. Label it, "Ham Curry with Noodles."

At Camp

Pour contents of Bag 1 into a bowl, add 4 cups of water and let it rehydrate for at least one hour.

Drain off the excess liquid, save it and add enough water to make four cups.

Boil enough water to cook the noodles and add contents of Bag 4. Remove from heat and cover while you make the sauce.

To make the sauce, melt the butter in a large pot. Stir in the ingredients from Bag 2. Slowly add the rehydration liquid and whisk until it thickens. Add contents of Bag 3 and cook over low heat. Stir constantly. Add contents of Bag 5 and Bag 1. Combine the sauce and noodles and serve immediately.

Judy and I are writing *The Long Ride Cookbook.* It is a book

69

for people who want to spend time camping and eating in the outdoors. Because we like to take pack trips we have included a section on how to do pack trips. The real purpose of this book is to encourage adventurers to travel light and still be able to enjoy great food. We know that a lot of cowboys are tough and don't mind carrying heavy Dutch ovens and iron frying pans, but we hope our cookbook will offer options to help all adventurers lighten their loads.

TIP: Looking for a way to soften your jerky? Do as cowboys used to do—put a hunk of jerky under your saddle and ride until it's soft enough to eat.

OUR FAVORITE HAM JERKY

Over the years people have asked me if they could use fresh pork to make jerky. I think it is wiser to use ham. To vary the flavor we have used both maple syrup and brown sugar as a substitute for the honey.

3/4 cup orange juice
1/2 cup honey
1/4 cup whiskey
1 teaspoon freshly ground black
    pepper

4 cups country ham strips

Mix the ingredients together, add ham, marinate at least 12 hours, then dry.

MOOSE JERKY

Verlen Krueger

At age 80 Verlen Krueger is a unique individual. He's an adventurer extraordinaire, a world-class canoeist who serves as an inspiration. Verlen didn't step into a canoe until he was 41 years old, but since then he's canoed more than 100,000 miles. It is a recorded fact that he has canoed more than anyone else in the world. He's canoed over 28,000 miles across the North American continent. He has gone up and down the Mississippi River and paddled from the Arctic Ocean to South America's Cape Horn. Verlen is one of the only people who canoed up the Grand Canyon—not down—up.

I heard about Verlen when a member of his support crew called to buy my book *Just Jerky* to make jerky for his next trip where he will canoe the full length of the Yukon River. That's a 2,040 mile trip on the water from Whitehorse to the Bering Sea.

"For a canoeist or any adventurer, jerky speaks for itself," Verlen said. "It is lightweight, it's full of protein, it doesn't break up in your pack and it keeps for a long time. When it's vacuum packed, it won't give off a scent for bears or other wildlife and that's a good thing."

Verlen had an incredible jerky-making experience while on one of his canoe trips. "We were way up in the Northwest Territories," he recalled. "We had just portaged up the Richardson

Mountain, paddled through a pass and came down a small creek. We were heading to Alaska. We'd made camp in a willow thicket along the sandy riverside, we had just set up our tents, had a fire going when we saw movements in the brush real close, in fact way too close to our campsite."

"It was a moose! It was completely unaware of us—four weary canoeists. Our guide, a Native American for whom moose are always in season, prepared his gun to shoot. We tried to talk him out of it, suggesting there'd be too much wasted meat. But he shot. His aim was true and we spent the rest of the night butchering."

The next morning the four men filled their two canoes with moose meat and paddled to the nearest village to trade moose meat for groceries. With the meat they kept, they cut long thin strips about $1/4$-inch thick, then rubbed the strips with salt and pepper and began the jerky making process over their campfire.

"Drying all that moose meat into jerky took three nights," Verlen said. "We'd dry it over the campfire at night, the next morning we'd wrap it up while we traveled during the day, then we'd hang it again at night."

"It tasted great," he recalled. "Since then, I love moose meat. It's better than steak, although it's hard to get and I'll probably never

have it that fresh again, since I don't generally carry a gun on my trips and I'm usually too busy canoeing to hunt or fish."

On this moose jerky trip along the voyageurs' fur trade route, he canoed 6,000 miles from Montreal to the Bering Sea. It was on this trip that he had his first encounter with native people drying fish in preparation for the long Arctic winter. When the four canoeists arrived in the Northwest Territories, just above the Arctic Circle, after the long days of the Arctic midsummer, which happened to be during the salmon run, they spotted racks of drying fish along the river banks.

"We were curious, so we stopped to talk to the people,"

Verlen remembered. "They told us that every year, as far back as they knew, their people caught and dried fish in exactly the same way." They used fish wheels to catch the salmon. A fish wheel has spokes placed over the river and when the spokes on the paddle turn it dips through the water and a bucket on another spoke traps the salmon. The bucket dumps the fish into another container. People take out the fish, slit them open and scrape out the innards with a serrated knife. With the whole fish intact, including the skin and head, they are hung on racks near a fire so that the smoke will keep any insects away, as well as dry and preserve the fish.

"Those folks showed us how to bite the meat away from the skin with their teeth," he said. "I was surprised that it tasted more smoky, than salty."

Since that experience Verlen tries to take dried fish along on his wilderness adventures whenever he can. "Dried fish balance our carbo-heavy diet," he said. "It was so great to get a new supply of dried fish on that trip because we didn't have any time for fishing. I was concentrating on canoeing—I wanted to do the entire route in one season, even though it took the voyageurs two. This had never been done before and we didn't have any time to waste."

In addition to eating jerky as a snack he also uses it in cooking.

After setting up camp and building a fire, he makes his all-time favorite dinner —macaroni and cheese with jerky.

VERLEN'S MAC 'N' CHEESY JERKY
3 cups water
2 cups macaroni noodles
½ cup jerky, fish or meat, cut in ¼-inch pieces
1 cup powdered cheese

Cook the macaroni in boiling water until it's tender, then drain and stir in the jerky and add the cheese.

GRRRMET JERKY PET TREATS

Stephanie Marcoux

Driving home from a job she hated, Stephanie Marcoux started making loud, deep-throated, growling sounds—"GRRRRRR!"

Just then she remembered a conversation she had with a friend, who had said somewhat flippantly, "Why don't you just sell those dog treats you make for Boots?"

"That's it!" Stephanie realized with a laugh, "And I'll call my business, GRRR."

She had been looking to start her own business, but up to that point nothing had felt right. A pet treat business, however, sounded just right—after all, it was a logical extension of her love for animals. Since that moment, the spelling of her business name has evolved to GRRRMET, and the sound of freedom still resonates for Stephanie.

TIP: "To anyone who has an idea and passion: don't give up too soon. Persistence pays off."

It all really began with Stephanie's love for her Border Collie, Boots, who got sick and needed a special diet.

"She was always spoiled, but after she developed cancer, her treats had to be special, too," Stephanie said. "Plain dried meat didn't tempt her and she had to eat, so I soaked thin strips of beef in soy sauce, honey and added a little garlic. Boots loved them. I don't know if those treats helped her live any longer, but I do know she died happy."

To set up her business in the state of Washington, all she needed was to get a $20 business license and to have insurance. Licensing for pet treats is a lot simpler than licensing for human jerky consumption. The only requirement she had was to make sure that her product labels clearly stated that her products were "For Pets."

"There are no governmental requirements for listing weight or ingredients," she explained. "Only Colorado and Massachusetts require weight and measure information on the packaging." However, Stephanie plays it safe and has her products analyzed and tested for protein, moisture, fat and fiber by Feed Laboratory in Trenton, New Jersey. "If we didn't do the testing it could be possible for someone to sue."

Stephanie soon found a ready market among her friends and their pets. For one friend whose dog was allergic to beef, Stephanie created a chicken jerky that she made from breast meat. "It dried to such a nice golden color which appealed to the pet's owner better than cheaper cuts that turned a dull, uninteresting brown."

Stephanie's husband, Will took on the tasks of cleaning out their garage. He installed blowers and air purifiers. He set up tables and built lots of storage racks. They bought a large freezer and six 30-tray food dehydrators. He installed two big sinks, then created a work surface to use as the cutting area and designated a container storage spot. Finally, they cleared a space for doing the packaging and keeping up with the bookwork.

Marketing was next. A friend suggested that they take their treats to dog and cat shows to learn about the industry and then after that to approach pet stores.

"Some of the best suggestions came from cat show people," Stephanie said. "Cat shows are really boring. Cats stay put in their cages, are taken out, evaluated and are put back in. The owners sit around and talk. One lady told me her cat adored fish and wondered if I could I make her little darling a special fish jerky?"

"That's where we got the idea of fish-flavored treats," Stephanie said. "Besides, cat people love to be testers. It was a win/win situation. I don't know what we would have done without such good, helpful friends."

"We cut everything by hand," she said with conviction. "I want nice $1/8$-inch uniform strips. We don't use any chemicals or preservatives in any of our marinades."

Stephanie buys top round for her beef treats and marinates the strips in light soy sauce, honey and garlic for three hours.

"I wear gloves when I take the meat strips out of the marinade to minimize the staining of my hands."

Each week a wholesale distributor delivers 40-pound boxes of frozen beef and boxes of chicken breasts. She lets the breasts thaw enough so they can easily be cut into narrow strips. She marinates the chicken strips in garlic and a Vietnamese anchovy extract that is typically used in Oriental cooking. "Its fishiness appeals to cats," she said. After marinating for three hours she dries the chicken until it is hard, then breaks it into little pieces, which is how cats prefer it.

"My advice is to shop around for the best prices. I've found that my local grocery store will sometimes give me a better price than the big-time suppliers."

It didn't take Stephanie long to decide she needed more products. She experimented with drying beef and chicken liver. "Frozen liver was a disaster. It turned to mush when it thawed," she recalled.

Her chicken and beef liver treats are simply cut and dried. "Beef liver becomes a shiny, dark brown when it dries," she said. But beware the smell. "Drying liver generates a very strong smell. It's a good thing our business is out in the country so the smells do not offend our neighbors. But I must admit we've attracted our share of animals."

When a holistic practioner told Stephanie that emu was good for animals with allergies she found a local emu rancher, visited, and came home with a whole emu carcass in her trunk. "Luckily, my husband's a good butcher and took care of that bird." She soon discovered that cats go insane over emu jerky.

"Both dogs and cats go wild for small pieces of dried shrimp and calamari (squid), too." Now Stephanie routinely receives 40-pound boxes of frozen, pre-cooked shrimp and frozen cala-mari from a wholesale seafood distributor.

"I have lots of stories about how much cats and dogs love my treats," she said. Her favorite story is one about a cat owner who woke during the night hear-ing dragging sounds across her wood floor. The cat owner sat up in bed and thought she saw her husband's pants going across the floor. Thinking she must be dreaming she lay down and went back to sleep. In the morning the pants were in the hall, the pocket was inside out and an empty shredded bag of GRRRMET treats was strewn about. Her husband had stuffed a package of calamari treats in his pocket, the cat crawled in, moved the pants across the floor and out of sight of the owner and devoured the treats." Stephanie laughed, "That proves that calamari jerky is irre-sistible. It does smell pretty fishy."

Another product—chicken, beef and lamb puffs—were her husband's brainchild. He's a mailman and he refuses to carry spray, instead he always has a pocketfull of Jerky Puffs. "They are crunchy, round ball pet treats that are about the size of a melon ball. They are dried as hard as lit-tle rocks," Stephanie said. "He likes them because they don't break up in his pocket and all the dogs love them. Why he's got one 11-year-old mutt that waits next to the mailbox and does flips when she sees him coming."

To make the puffs, after cleaning the meat they grind it only enough that it is chunky. The lamb puffs are made from leg of lamb, cooked brown rice, shredded raw carrots, a little sea salt and vegetable bouillon. The bouillon provides enough moisture to hold the puffs together. Chicken and beef puffs contain cooked white rice, shredded raw carrots, sea salt and bouillon. Stephanie mixes the ingredients together then uses a melon baller as a scoop, then dries these little balls.

Her six dehydrators, set at 155 degrees, all run constantly. A leather sheet on the bottom tray protects the dehydrator base from drips. She uses mesh screens when drying shrimp or any other small pieces to prevent small pieces from falling through, and to prevent chicken liver from wrapping around the spokes of the drying tray. Most of her prod-ucts dry overnight, although pre-cooked shrimp dries faster. Liver treats take about 12 hours.

GRRRMET pet jerky treats are sold in stores from New York to California and her wholesale business is booming. The pet treat brand Pooch Party Mix uses her dried liver as one of its ingredients. Unlike many new businesses, Stephanie abandoned her web site because, "It created too many small orders. With processing, packaging and the charge for charging, it ate up too much time for too little profit," she said.

ALASKAN SALMON JERKY

Sandro Lane

The only thing Sandro Lane did-not tell me about his salmon jerky business was how much salt he added to his brine. "I'll give you a clue," he said. "Take a fresh, unpeeled potato, stick a 10-penny nail in it, drop the potato in a gal-lon of water, add salt and stir constantly. Stop adding salt when the potato floats. That's how you start to make a good brine. Always keep track of the amount of salt you've added, then when you make jerky, note if it tastes too salty or not salty enough. With the next batch, add more or less, or cut the brining time in half. You can control the saltiness by either shortening or lengthen-ing the brining time or by reduc-ing or strengthening the brine."

I have been making jerky for years, but I have to admit, fish jerky had been a problem for me until I understood that you don't need as much salt as is called for in many traditional brine/mari-nade recipes. After I reduced the amount of salt I found that fish jerky can be absolutely delicious.

Sandro went to Alaska in 1978 to work as a marine biolo-gist. It didn't take him long to decide he wasn't cut out to be a government worker, but he had fallen in love with Juneau and didn't want to leave.

"I'd gotten pretty good at catching fish, but I got even better at smoking them," he chuckled. "For years I'd lived in Italy where they cold-smoke lox. I started

81

Sandro Lane holding soon-to-be salmon jerky.

messing around and came up with a really good lox-making technique, then I learned the basic process of curing meat and making salami. I put the two together and came up with my salmon jerky."

After converting his garage into a food processing plant in 1984 he perfected a cold-smoking technique for making Alaskan salmon jerky. When he received a U.S. Small Business Administration loan for his business, Taku Smokeries, he moved to a larger building. With the move to the downtown Juneau waterfront in 1992, Taku Smokeries occupied more than three acres, with more than 40,000 square feet of warehouse space. The two companies,

Taku Smokeries and Taku Fisheries, process over six million pounds of fish annually and in 2000 did $20 million worth of business. Although the bulk of their products are sold to domestic and foreign wholesale markets, they keep the best quality fresh fish for themselves. "This gives us an advantage over any of the other salmon jerky competitors," Sandro said.

"What does Taku mean?" I asked.

"It's the Tlingit Indian name for the bitter cold wind that can reach 90 miles an hour that blows through the Southeastern Alaskan Taku River Valley."

Salmon fishing begins by the third Sunday in June and ends in early October. Sandro explained that there are five different species of salmon. Each has its own characteristics and each is known by two names. "The King is the most oily and is also known as chinook. The King becomes too rubbery to use for jerky. The sockeye, also called red, is generally smoked. The coho is also called the silver. The pink or humpback is so small there is nothing to filet. Taku Smokeries uses the keta, also called chum, to make their jerky. It contains 4 to 5 percent fat, which is less than the other types so it dries better," he said.

Salmon jerky starts with a de-headed and gutted fish that's been filleted and placed in a brine. "Our brine time is measured in hours, not days—usually 12 hours and we do not put it in the refrigerator," Sandro stated.

The brined salmon is quickly frozen, then cut lengthwise with a band saw, creating $1/4$-inch wide strips as long as possible. While still frozen the strips are hung on racks in the smokehouse. A light alder wood smoke is applied for 12 to 16 hours. "It takes 1,000 pounds of live chum to make 150 pounds of deep red, paper-thin, original or peppered salmon jerky."

"All the racking and packaging is done by hand," he said. "Our salmon is different from most other salmon jerky. Others grind fish, extrude the ground fish through a nozzle, then dry it on a flat sheet. It is cut in small pieces, then packaged."

Taku salmon jerky is flavored only with alder smoke and salt. There are no preservatives, no binders and no colors or flavors are added." Jerky dried at higher temperatures gets brittle," Sandro said. "My preference is to dry slower at a low temperature that never gets above 90 degrees. This process produces a softer jerky although it requires refrigeration after it is dried." To make their jerky shelf-stable would require adding nitrates or flushing it with nitrogen gas. "I think that would ruin our product," he said.

"Our cold water salmon is good for you," Sandro said brightly. "It is the best and most natural source and the highest concentration of Omega-3 oil."

According to the Alaskan Seafood web site, "Omega-3 oils produce a series of eicosanoids that have been shown to decrease the risk for heart disease, reduce inflammation, and positively impact certain cancers."

"Our cold smoking process keeps the Omega-3 integrity, whereas high temperatures denature its benefits," Sandro reported.

Sandro feels that one of his company's biggest accomplishments is that the Japanese are his best customers. "They eat the most fish of any group on our planet, they have the most knowledge and the highest standards," Sandro explained with pride.

GOLD STAR EFFORT

I give this company a gold star for environmental awareness. Taku ships all of its products in insulated styrofoam boxes. To keep the styrofoam out of landfills, they ask their customers to send the box back to their company. Then on the customer's next order, Taku reimburses the amount the customer spent on postage.

"Our salmon comes from the unspoiled waters of Southeast Alaska and our business is dependent on a clean environment," Sandro said. "We feel this policy just makes good sense."

A TROPHY HUNTER

Lee Hofer

"In as much as three-quarters of the earth's surface is water and only one quarter is land, the good Lord's intentions are clear," Lee Hofer stated with both humor and conviction. "A man's time should be divided accordingly—three-quarters for hunting and fishing, and one quarter for work."

Lee has hunted all over the world and you can see evidence of his hunting prowess in his shop, Lee's Meat & Sausage in Tea, South Dakota. More than 125 mounts, including bear, musk ox, caribou, buffalo, bobcats, antelope, wild turkey, paddlefish, salmon, sailfish and more are on display there. Plus, he got a lot of them with a bow and arrows—not bullets. "I prefer archery to a gun," he said.

When he leaned over the counter and cocked his head in my direction, I knew a favorite adventure was ready to roll off his tongue.

"It was 75 below and the morning of our second day on Nunivik Island in Alaska," he said. "The night before, we'd dug a hole in the deep snow, lined it with thick, black plastic bags, covered the top with more plastic and spent the night breathing through a straw so we wouldn't breathe in our own moist air and freeze our lungs."

"My guide said sternly, 'Today you use your 338 Winchester'.

I'd insisted on using my bow

85

and arrow the day before, and with so much clothing on I'd had a hard time taking aim. I took his advice and when I pulled the trigger I downed a 600-pound musk ox with nice big horns. We butchered it right on the spot, then loaded it on sleds that were hooked behind our snowmobiles."

"Let me tell you, musk ox is good no matter what you do with it, but the jerky was absolutely incredible. I removed all the fat and cut it into $1/2$-inch strips. I rubbed each strip with Morton's™ smoke-flavored sugar cure, dried it, then painted each side with A-1™ sauce and dried it again," he said.

At Lee's Meat & Sausage, he has three computerized, stainless steel smokehouses that are 7 feet high and 4 feet square. In each one, 1,000 pounds of meat can be smoked at one time. He uses a blend of three different hardwoods, with hickory dominant. Small wood pieces go in a stainless steel box on the side that automatically turns and drops the wood on a hot plate, the smoke goes in the smokehouse, the dampers open and for about $2^1/2$ hours, the meat is flooded with smoke.

"In 1983, we took our products to be judged at the International Meat Trade Fair in Germany. Our dried and cured beef took second place in world competition. Every product that we have has taken a first in some competition," he said proudly.

"My life goal was to combine my love of hunting and my work. And I've done it!"

WILD TURKEY JERKY
"A wild 20-pound turkey has about 4 pounds of breast meat and generally we get another pound off the legs. We slice strips $1/4$-inch-thick and as long as we can," Lee said.

$1/2$ cup honey
4 tablespoons Morton Tender Quick
4 teaspoons brown sugar
2 teaspoon liquid smoke
2 teaspoon black pepper
2 teaspoon onion powder

4 pounds wild turkey breast strips
Mix the ingredients in a bowl, then pour over the turkey strips. Cover and let set overnight in the refrigerator. Stir one more time, then put in a drying environment of at least 160 degrees.

BEAR JERKY

"Bear is the only animal you hunt that you should really just take the hide and go," Lee claimed. "However, if you want to make bear jerky, take the back strap and the hind quarters. Don't bother with the front quarters because they're marbled with too much fat. You can tell by the black bear's skin if it has parasites—you can see the pit-ting effect inside the skin."

1/4 cup soy sauce
1/4 cup Worcestershire sauce
1 teaspoon salt
1 teaspoon liquid smoke
1 teaspoon onion powder
1/2 teaspoon monosodium glutamate
1/3 teaspoon garlic powder
1/3 teaspoon ground black pepper

1 1/2 pounds semi-frozen bear strips

Slice the bear steak diagonally, across the grain, into 1/4-inch-thick strips. Combine seasoning mixture and brush it on both sides of the strips, then arrange them on two 10 by 15-inch jelly roll pans. Place in a preheated, 200 degree oven for eight to 12 hours. Leave the oven door slightly ajar to allow moisture to escape. Turn strips several times during the drying process to assure it evenly dries. It makes about a half pound of jerky that's dark, black and chewy. This formula can also be used with ground bear meat.

TIP: If you have a home vacuum packer, put the bear strips and the marinade in a plastic bag and draw a vacuum. Then work the pouch by hand, let it set and work it again. "You'll be surprised at what a great product this produces," Lee said.

CARP JERKY

Mike Schafer

Mike owns Schafer Fisheries in Fulton, Illinois, on the Mississippi River across from Clinton, Iowa, at the U. S. Lock and Dam #13, 50 miles south of Dubuque.

When *Big River* Magazine published an article called "Camp Kielbasa" in April, 1997 Mike was beginning to develop his carp jerky. "That article gave me incentive to go forward," he said. "Now it's our main jerky and it's real hard to keep on hand. It took me three years to develop a carp

jerky I could eat. I kept trying new brines and different woods for smoking. Plus it took a sizeable financial investment to get the right equipment."

On Tuesday, September 11, 2001, Mike Schafer was sitting in his boat, fishing for carp on the Mississippi when his cell phone rang. Picking it up, his wife's voice cracked, "Something terrible has happened in New York City." There was a long pause, "Two planes hit the World Trade

Center towers," she cried.

Just like everyone else Mike's main concern was for the people in those buildings and planes. Then he remembered he had two shipments of fresh fish and carp jerky scheduled for delivery to his New York City delicatessen customers that morning. "My heart stopped when I realized my drivers were in Manhattan during the attack," he said. "Minutes later his drivers called to report they were safe.

89

However, Mike did lose two hard-earned loads of the Mississippi's finest fish, although the carp jerky survived.

"Jerky is a delicious snack food," Mike said. "If we ever find ourselves without electricity, it could become a survival food real fast."

Each batch starts with about 500 pounds of carp filets. After brining he uses maple and fruit woods to smoke the carp. "I don't use hickory because it makes jerky too dark." Every thirty minutes he checks the temperature in his gas fired smokehouse. "Jerky must reach an internal temperature of at least 145 degrees so I keep my eyes on it," he said. "Depending on the humidity, sometimes a batch can take two days to finish."

Mike is looking for new ways to expand his business and is considering getting a fish deboner to process the Asian carp that was planted in 1993 in Arkansas and Mississippi ponds in an attempt to control algae. "During the floods it began to infiltrate the whole river. Some people feel it's a potential problem; however if there was some way to bring them to market it could be a positive thing. Although it's similar in taste to the Chinese or the Bighead carp, the Asian looks entirely different and has white meat fish whereas regular carp is red. It takes regular carp about 10 years to reach 25 pounds and sometimes the Asian gets that big in four years. I figure since there is a world-wide need for protein, this fish could feed a whole lot of people."

THE JERKY LINK

Jack Link

A sign standing halfway between main street Minong, Wisconsin and the Link Snack headquarters and plant/processing facility reads, "Ordinary People Doing the Extraordinary."

The Link jerky making company is a beehive of activity. This is particularly impressive in a world of lay-offs, plant closings, shattered loyalties and compromised expectations. "Everyone works hard," Jack Link, CEO said. "Our success is a result of customer and employee loyalty, plus a lot of hard work, soap and water."

The impact of this jerky business on the little northern Wisconsin town has been monumental. While dot-coms have cooked themselves into vapor, the Link Company represents another family-owned and managed company that has provided growth and jobs since 1984. Link has been the number one jerky supplier to America's convenience, grocery and drug stores nationwide with their red, white and blue packages of jerky.

Interestingly, their story is not unique. It runs consistent throughout the jerky world. Sons following in Dad's footsteps.

Is it something about cutting meat, or is it about wanting to work hard? Or is it simply family loyalty? What ever it is, it works, and not only for the immediate family, but for the larger community as well.

Chris Link, Jack's grandfather, settled in Minong in the 1890's and worked on the thriving railroad and bought and sold cattle. "Grandpa had a sixth sense for cattle, in a split second he could pick out the best," Jack said.

Chris's son, Earl operated a stock farm, owned a feed, grocery and hardware store, and ran a meat market.

Wolf, Earl's brother went west every week to buy horses until 1938, when folks began using horses less. So Wolf became one of the biggest Allis Chalmer machinery dealers in the country. Eventually he opened a Ford dealership, an appliance store and in 1972 he built a meat packing plant and processed about 550 cows per day. By the mid-80s they supplied McDonald's with meat.

One fall day Jack and his sons, Troy and Jay were going hunting and they stopped at a convenience store and bought some jerky. Throughout the day they gnawed on that tough jerky. The light bulb went on—with their family knowledge of meat processing and sausage-making they could make much better jerky. Their goal was to make a jerky that was moister and more tender.

After submitting their first package of jerky to the U.S.D.A., they were told it could not be called "jerky" because of its higher moisture content. In time the U.S.D.A. gave them permission to call their new meat snack, "kippered beef steak."

"Most convenience store operators didn't know what "kippered" meant," Jack commented.

"Is it fish?" they'd ask.

Eventually, consumers loved it and demanded more flavors and within a few years they had a multi-million dollar snack food business.

Like Colonel Sanders, Jack Link is protective of his recipes, but recommends that jerky makers always use the freshest and highest quality ingredients they can find.

JERKY JUDGE'S RECIPE

Monte Carlson

In the early seventies Monte Carlson bought his first food dehydrator specifically to make jerky. Over the years he tinkered with various recipes and until he started making the Kevin and Annie recipe from *Just Jerky,* a smoky jerky marinade was his favorite.

He used the smoky marinade when one of his pals shot an antelope with his bow. He made jerky out of the whole of it. Of course, he took a third of the jerky for his services as jerky maker. "Antelope meat is not very good, but antelope jerky is great," he said.

SMOKY JERKY MARINADE
1 1.25 oz. package McCormick Meat Marinade Mix™
1 tablespoon liquid smoke
1 tablespoon olive oil
1 cup water
1 teaspoon salt
Lots of grated orange peeling

4 pounds of meat strips

Mix the packaged marinade according to its directions. Put in a large self-sealing plastic freezer bag. Add liquid smoke, oil, salt, orange peel and let stand for 30 minutes. Add water, mix and let stand 30 more minutes. Then add meat. Soak at least two hours (overnight is better). Occasionally squeeze the plastic bag. Drain, place on drying trays and dry at 145 degrees.

A JERKY CRIME: A TRUE STORY

These are the documented facts as contained in both the public file and in the written opinion.

A federal USDA Compliance Officer in Spokane, Washington stopped his vehicle at a roadside retail stand that was selling flowers and jerky and purchased 20 pounds of beef jerky.

He submitted some of the jerky to a lab for analysis. The lab reported that the jerky contained deer (and pork) and was not "beef" as labeled. He then traced the jerky from the roadside retailer, through an Idaho gun show, to The End of the Road Packing Company in Burley, Idaho.

The Officer then bought another 10 pounds. Again a lab test revealed the jerky was made from venison and not beef.

Mislabeling food products is a federal crime. Buying or selling wild game or parts of wild game is a crime in Idaho. The End of the Road Company is a domestic meat processing plant and did not have the right to purchase or sell wild game meat.

While the USDA Compliance Officer and the Idaho Department of Fish and Game investigated the meat packing company and its owners, the sheriff's office was also doing its own investigation of the business and its owners, but for a different reason—illegal drugs.

It seems the county bank had twice notified the sheriff's office of a funny smelling cash deposit made by one of the packing plant's owners. In fact, twice a cash line up was performed and twice a drug dog "indicated" on the money deposited by the owner. On both occasions the money smelled like marijuana to the sheriff's officer.

All law enforcement agencies began working together, but friction soon arose. The USDA and the Idaho Department of Fish and Game wanted immediately to seek a search warrant to see if the meat packing plant was involved in a poaching operation and/or in the purchase or sale of illegal game. However, the sheriff's office wanted to wait until they could either get an informer into the meat packing plant or else make a controlled drug buy from one of the owners. A turf battle ensued.

Then without consent or notice to the sheriff's office, and while the chief sheriff's deputy assigned to the case was in Virginia, the Idaho Department of Fish and Game applied to a magistrate for a search warrant. The magistrate issued the warrant.

There were many potential problems with the search warrant, one of them being time—ninety three days had passed from the date of the USDA Compliance Officer's purchase of the illegal jerky to the date of the search warrant. Was this 93-day old evidence too stale?

When the search warrant was executed, the officers entered the meat packing plant and found 45 untagged deer (actually 89 hindquarters). In addition, inside the meat packing warehouses they found a virtual marijuana farm, with lights, drying equipment, growing plants, etc.

The owners challenged the magistrate's decision to issue the search warrant. One of their claims was that the evidence before the magistrate was too stale—too much time had elapsed from the jerky production, to the gun show, to the flower and jerky vendor, to the jerky purchase by the Federal USDA Officer, until finally the search warrant.

A valid search warrant must be based upon "probable cause" that the items sought, will actually be at the place to be searched, at the time of the search. The probability that the items will still be there is lessened by the passage of time. *Sgro v. United States, 287 U.S. 206 (1932).*

For example, the observation of a half-smoked marijuana cigarette in an ashtray at a cocktail party may be stale the day after the cleaning lady has been in; while the observation of the burial of a corpse in a cellar may well not be stale three decades later. *Andersen v. State, 331 A. 2d 78 (1975).*

The District Judge, Monte B. Carlson, ruled that evidence of meat products, vacuum packaged or frozen, jerky or salami, should not be considered stale simply by counting days. Speaking specifically to the facts of that case, he wrote: "In this case we are dealing with products such as jerky and salami, which by their very nature are durable. The very reason meat is made into jerky or salami is to preserve it by removing the moisture and curing it."

The case is on appeal.

Some questions remain:

What was there about the taste of this jerky that caused the USDA Compliance Officer to buy 20 pounds?

Were all or only a few strips sent to the lab?

What was it about this jerky that caused the Officer to go back for another 10 pounds?

Why did the lab need to do more than one analysis?

Just how many "scientific samples" were necessary and why? *(There were rumors that this was really great tasting jerky.)*

What was it about this jerky that caused a turf *("grass")* battle among the different law enforcement agencies?

And finally, was the combined smell of jerky and pot too much for the drug dog to discriminate?

ALLIGATOR JERKY

The Loesch Brothers

"You gotta include alligator jerky!" said my friend Ira Newman when I called one day to talk about his design for the cover of this book.

"Well, Ira," I said, "You're the one who lives in Florida. You should write about it."

"Stake a medium-sized dog on the 15th fairway just west of Miami," he began.

I roared with laughter. "Your first line alone is worth the story."

"Just kidding," he went on. "You know, at one time everybody was killing alligators, then they became protected and lots of alligator farms emerged. Since alligators lay about 40 eggs at a time it didn't take long for the population to re-establish itself and now we've got a thriving alligator community. With all the farms and wild gators, people really are losing their dogs and cats."

Ira set out on a taste-testing mission and returned convinced that the smoked alligator from the Arawak Lobster & Fish Market was the best he'd found. The owners and brother's, Gregg, Jack and Kerry Loesch run their Miami, Florida based business.

"What convinced me that I'd chosen the right place was a sign hanging in the store. "Our alligator filets are marinated for four days in a sauce of honey, brown sugar, molasses, garlic, scotch bonnet and many more herbs and spices. Don't bother to copy," the sign advised. "It took us 30 years to develop."

A 200-pound, six- to eight-foot alligator has about 50 pounds of meat in its tail. After skinning the tail and cutting three-quarter-inch steaks, the brothers cut it lengthwise to make their filets. Then they use a large wooden mallet to tenderize the meat.

After marinating, the fillets are placed over an oak smolder—not a fire—for four to five hours, depending on the thickness of the meat.

"Let me tell you," Ira said, "These guys have perfected a marinade and smoke combination that will make anyone sit up straight."

Smoked alligator is still a step away from jerky.

"To turn alligator filets into jerky just add a preservative to the marinade," Gregg said, and his opinion was seconded by his brother Jack.

The Arawak Lobster & Fresh Fish Market.

POSSUM JERKY

Neil Haugerud

Every other Tuesday morning I meet up with a couple writing buddies, Neil Haugerud is a former Minnesota sheriff and author of *Jailhouse Stories,* and Al Mathison who's a darn good storyteller. We get together to drink coffee, to share our literary dreams and aspirations and to boost each other up. One day, Neil was going on about a trip to Louisiana that he'd just returned from. At one point he raised one arm, left the other looking like it was resting on a Bible and swore the story he was about to tell us was the whole truth and nothing but.

"While in the process of sliding some fresh-shucked, raw oysters down my gullet, devouring a platter of peeled shrimp and simultaneously enjoying a small libation at my sister's house in Baton Rouge, Louisiana, I turned to her and asked, 'Monica, have you ever heard of anyone who makes possum or alligator jerky?'

"Before she could reply, her friend Kathy spoke up.

"'My daddy used to be sheriff here in East Feliciana Parish,'" she said with a slow southern sweetness. 'Why he made the best baked possum I ever tasted.' She smacked her lips. 'Daddy kept a cage in the back yard and told all the high school boys that whenever they came across a possum they were to put it in that cage.' She looked around slyly. As she took her glance smoothly past me we both knew she had captured my complete attention. 'Daddy would feed those possums table scraps for about two weeks to get them nice and fat.'"

"'We've got the recipe in our cookbook,' Monica said."

"Cookbook, I said."

"'Yes,' Kathy said, coquettishly lowering her chin. 'My friends and I from the East Feliciana Pilgrimage and Garden Club published *Feliciana's Favorites*.'"

Monica brought the book and Kathy opened it right at her daddy's recipe.

"Here it is, as contributed by Arch V. Doughty, Sheriff, East Feliciana Parish, she said."

BAKED POSSUM A' LA FELIXVILLE
1 fat possum, cleaned well
12 medium sweet potatoes
2 medium onions, chopped
2 garlic cloves, minced
Red and black pepper
Salt to taste

Preparation of Possum
Feed possum table scraps for two weeks. Keep container of fresh water in cage. When ready to kill the animal—DO NOT SHOOT! Shooting brings blood to the surface, which will wet hair and make the possum hard to clean. Instead, hold possum by tail, place head on ground, place broom handle on neck, stand on each end of broom handle and pull up on tail until neck is broken. You will feel body give when neck breaks. When possum stops kicking, you are ready to clean.

To Clean
Make sure hair is dry. Hold possum over low outdoor fire and allow hair to singe. A large clothespin on your nose may make this task more pleasant. Burn and scrape until all hair is burned off down to the skin. Do not allow possum to stay in one position over the fire for too long. This will cause the skin to break. Turn the possum regularly and scrape it with a knife. After all the hair has been scraped off, use soap, warm water and a

cloth to wash thoroughly. Continue washing until body becomes white. Rinse well—be sure all soap is off. Using a sharp knife, cut off the feet, head and tail. Cut the body open on belly side and remove all entrails.

To Cook

Place the possum in a pot with enough water to cover. Season with onion, garlic, salt, red and black pepper (surface of water should be black and covered with pepper). Boil it, covered, until tender when pierced with a fork. Allow meat to cool in water. Partially bake the sweet potatoes, which have been rubbed with cooking oil, then peel them and place them in a cooking pan. Remove possum from water and place on top of the potatoes, skin side up. Bake at 350 degrees until outside skin is crusty brown. This is good eating.

NEIL'S POSSUM JERKY INSTRUCTIONS

Having passed along this gem of a recipe, Neil elaborated on his favorite method of making possum jerky:

"Go to the nearest liquor store, buy a case of beer or a large bottle of liquor. On second thought, buy both. Invite a friend over—not too close a friend. Open a beer or make a strong drink. Consume it while waiting for the friend. When the friend arrives, offer her/him a drink and have another yourself. Freshen drink often while proceeding through the preparation and cleaning process detailed in the above recipe. When you approach the part where it says, "'Using a sharp knife, cut off feet, head and tail,'" call another friend to perform this task. Tell stories and have drinks while waiting for the second friend. Proceed as above. When the possum is baked, cut it into 1/4-inch strips and prepare as you would any other jerky."

MY JERKY SUGGESTIONS

Mary Bell

While writing this book, I kept making notes of things I thought might be helpful. Hopefully this section will supplement the jerky people's stories and provide some worthwhile "how to" advice, recipes and tips.

Making jerky is easy and fun. In some way, when I make jerky I feel more connected with the past. I think about how Native Americans made Pemmican. Making jerky connects me to the wandering of Lewis and Clark who observed the way Native American's dried buffalo strips by hanging them from peeled willow branches and placing them in a windy, hot spot.

Jerky can be made from any muscle, but it is most often made from beef or wild game. Lean meat, poultry or fish is cut into strips, or ground, flavored, then dried. Strip jerky is made by cutting hunks of meat either with or against the grain to make strips about $1/4$-inch thick. Ground jerky is made with any ground protein, like hamburger. Flavors are added, then it's shaped and dried.

Jerky-making variables include: the type of meat, the size and thickness of the raw product, the combination of flavoring ingredients used in the marinade, cure or brine, the length of marinating/brining time, how it's dried, or smoked, for how long and at what temperature.

Drying concentrates the flavor, changes the texture and appearance, eliminates moisture and preserves it. Making your own jerky saves money and gives you control over the quality of the jerky because you can choose to use or not to use preservatives, as well as color and flavor enhancers.

SAFETY

There are three factors in making jerky safe to eat. First it's dried at a temperature of at least 145 degrees. This temperature is hot enough to kill most bacteria. Second, drying eliminates more than 90 percent of its water, which is the medium that bacteria need to reproduce. Third, by using one teaspoon of salt per pound of meat, the salt serves as a preservative when the jerky is dry.

USDA Safety: The USDA Meat and Poultry Hotline recommends to make jerky, that the meat must reach a temperature of at least 160 degrees. After reaching that temperature a constant temperature of 130 to 140 degrees. must be maintained during the drying process. In addition, the USDA requires that the drying process must be fast enough to dry the meat before it spoils and must remove enough water that microorganisms will not grow.

ABOUT FLAVORING

Jerky flavoring combinations are limitless. My best advice is to experiment!

A marinade is simply a sauce in which raw strips are soaked. Marinating adds flavor and sometimes acts as a method of tenderizing meat. A brine has a base of very salty water (pure is best) with flavorings added. Marinades are most often used with meat and poultry and brines are typically used with fish.

Earthenware crocks or glass bowls with covers are my first choice as marinating containers. Self-sealing plastic bags also work very well because you can squeeze out any excess air. Then by simply picking up the bag and turning it, you push the marinade around. So instead of having to stir the meat and marinade in a bowl to make sure all the pieces receive the benefit of the pretreatment—just give the bag a squeeze.

Caution—never re-use a

marinade because blood leaches into it.

Note that if you use the same size pieces they will dry in the same amount of time.

TIP: Washing meat, fish and poultry helps delay spoiling and get rid of any surface slime.

MARINADES AND BRINES

I've listed several potential ingredients for you to concoct your own marinade or brine. Do not be surprised if you use far more seasoning than you think necessary. Note that fish and poultry are more delicate than red meat, which means the flavorings penetrate faster and add more flavor.

Each ingredient listed is for one pound of meat, fish or poultry.

SALT: 1 TEASPOON

Salt is the most common brine and marinade ingredient.

Salt, sodium chloride ($NaCl$), is as essential to human life as sun and water. Its function is to maintain our equilibrium of liquids. We are in more danger of dehydration without salt than by not having water.

As a brine ingredient, salt draws water from muscle cells and at the same time it is absorbed by osmosis throughout the muscle tissue. Salt halts the action of harmful bacteria, inhibits enzyme growth and prevents spoilage by serving as a preservative. Too little

salt may result in spoilage and too much can create a hard, dry, over-salty, inedible jerky.

As a general rule, a brine requires one part salt to three parts water. Salt does not penetrate as rapidly in a fatty fish. A finely ground salt will penetrate flesh more rapidly.

SWEETENERS: 1 TABLESPOON

White or brown sugar is the most commonly used. Corn syrup, molasses, maple syrup and honey are also good choices.

LIQUID SMOKE: 1/4 TO 1/2 TEASPOON

Hickory is the most popular, although many other flavors are available in stores.

HERBS: 2 TEASPOONS FRESH OR 1 TEASPOON DRIED

Again, the potential is limitless. My favorite herbs are dill, oregano, marjoram, basil, cilantro and thyme. An option is to steep the herbs like a tea and add it to the marinade or brine.

SPICE: 1/4 TO 1/2 TEASPOON

Use ground or powdered garlic, cayenne, chili powder, cloves or allspice.

TENDERIZERS: 1/2 TEASPOON

Tenderizers separate connective tissues, which results in better flavor and increased tenderness, especially in old, tough, gamey meat. Evenly sprinkle at 1-inch intervals on the surface of the raw strips. Pierce strips with a fork so the tenderizer can penetrate as deeply as possible, then refrigerate for 12 hours.

VINEGAR: 1/8 CUP

Dr. Larry Borchert's theory about using vinegar to help meat reach its lowest water holding capacity and dry better and faster is in "A Proven Jerky Theory." Any vinegar will do.

ALCOHOL: 1/4 CUP

Although any kind of alcohol will lose its effect during drying, it adds great flavor.

JUICES: 1/4 CUP

Instead of water, substitute any fruit or vegetable juice.

COMMERCIAL SAUCES: 1 TABLESPOON

Soy sauce is made from fermented soybeans. Kikkoman, a preservative-free soy sauce, should be kept refrigerated once opened. Kikkoman also has a low-salt version that is reduced from 15 to 9 percent. La Choy™ or Chun King™ are synthetically produced from hydrolyzed vegetable protein, syrup and caramel. Shoyu and tamari are also soy sauces. Don't forget Tabasco and Worcestershire sauces.

COMMERCIAL PRODUCTS

In addition to Dean Clark's HI-MOUNTAIN™ spices and the American Harvest/Nesco Original Spice™ mixes that are mentioned in this book, there are a vast array of commercial spices on the market. Just remember to accurately weigh the meat, measure the curing ingredients and use the recommended proportions. Two popular seasoning products are Morton's Tender Quick, which is a combination of salt, sodium nitrite, sodium nitrate and sugar, and Accent. which contains Monosodium Glutamate (MSG) and is a flavor enhancer.

AN ORIGINAL JERKY TWIST

For three decades I've used a dehydrator to dry an enormous variety of food and that includes a generous share of jerky. My dehydrator has had many incarnations, at first it was called the Marvelizer, then it became the Companion, next the PressAireizer and now it's called the Gardenmaster. It's basically the same unit that was given new names although it was always manufactured by American Harvest—that is until the Metal Ware Corporation, manufacturers of Nesco Roasters—purchased American Harvest in 1997 and relocated it to Two Rivers, Wisconsin. The company is now called Nesco/American Harvest.

One of the company's most popular products has been the "original" spice. Of course, their formula is a well-guarded secret, so over the years I've played around, attempting to duplicate it. When I used the following combination of ingredients, my family thought I had used their original spice packet. I believe it's the peppercorn combination that did the trick.

Their seasoning packets include dextrose, salt, natural spices, hickory smoked flavor, onion powder, garlic powder, monosodium glutamate, hydrolyzed vegetable protein, and imitation maple flavor. The cure packet contains salt and sodium nitrate.

MY ORIGINAL VERSION

¼ cup soy sauce

2 tablespoons brown sugar

2 tablespoons white sugar

1 tablespoon liquid smoke

1 tablespoon finely ground pepper

1 tablespoon salt

1 teaspoon onion powder

1 teaspoon garlic powder

½ teaspoon finely ground pink
peppercorns

¼ teaspoon freshly ground green
peppercorns

¼ teaspoon freshly ground white
peppercorns

1 pound ground meat

Mix all the ingredients together,
then add the ground meat. Let sit
at least an hour, although it's better when it marinates longer.
Form and dry at 145 degrees.

CURT'S VARIATION

Executive vice-president, Curt
Drumm, who is also the son of
the owner, offered one of his
original spice variations.

2 packages Nesco/American
Harvest Original Spice™

1 packet Nesco/American Harvest
Cure™

2 tablespoons soy sauce

2 tablespoons Worcestershire
sauce

1 tablespoon tomato sauce

1 tablespoon water

1 teaspoon minced garlic

½ teaspoon ground pepper

3 pounds ground meat

Mix all the ingredients together,
add ground meat and marinate at
least 1 hour in the refrigerator.
Shape and dry at 145 degrees.

VACUUM IT

For those who own a home vacuum packer, put the strips and the marinade in either a bag or a jar, (a jar is best) and pull a vacuum. The force of the vacuum pushes the marinade into the raw strips. This will shorten the marinating time by thoroughly distributing the marinade through-out the cells tissues.

BRUSH IT

After any type of strips have been placed in any drying environment and the surface moisture has dried off, dip a brush into a bowl of molasses, honey or barbecue sauce. Then simply apply a thin coating to the surface of the meat. If you mix a little warm water with the coating it will be easier to spread.

SPRAY IT

Get a spray atomizer. Then make any kind of herb tea. Add
1 teaspoon garlic powder
1 teaspoon liquid smoke
    Give the ingredients a whirl in a blender or stir well. Then pour in a spray atomizer bottle and spray the top and bottom of any meat, fish or poultry slices during the drying process.

DO A DOUBLE-DIP

If a jerky has been dried too hard, or has too little flavor, or it's just simply a failure and you want to fix it, try double-dip drying. Bad jerky is tough, gritty or tastes burnt. Take that bad jerky and soak for just a couple minutes in a simple marinade, then dry it again. It has been my experience that this has not only rescued a failed jerky, but has resulted in some really great jerky.

DO A TWO-STEP

To impart even more flavor, first rub a dry cure into the strips, place in a container for at least 24 hours, remove, drain and wash. Then make your favorite marinade, add the strips and marinate for at least one hour, remove and dry.

111

DRY CURES

Dry cures are combinations of salt, sugar and flavorings that are applied directly to the surface of meat, fish or poultry strips. Strips are laid in a single layer on a clean flat surface, liberally sprinkled on both sides, then with your hands the cure is thoroughly rubbed into all surfaces. The strips are placed in a covered glass or earthenware container and refrigerated at least 12 hours.

A cure helps kill bacteria. Many cures contain the curing salt, sodium nitrite ($NaNO_2$), or sodium nitrate ($NaNO_3$). Sodium nitrite is a very powerful, and potentially dangerous, naturally occurring chemical. If too much enters the human body it can be toxic. The United States Department of Agriculture requires using only 6.1 grams of sodium nitrite to cure 100 pounds of meat. Sodium nitrite inhibits Clostridium botulinum spore growth, provides the typical pink color of cured meat, adds flavor and assists in preventing oxidation.

MY FAVORITE DRY CURE

1 tablespoon salt

1 teaspoon sugar

1 teaspoon crushed cumin seeds

½ teaspoon curry powder

½ teaspoon ground ginger

¼ teaspoon garlic powder

¼ teaspoon ground, black pepper

⅛ teaspoon cinnamon

⅛ teaspoon ground cloves

2 pounds meat strips

Combine the ingredients. Sprinkle on the strips. Cover, let sit at least 12 hours, then drain and dry.

MAKING STRIP JERKY

Choose good quality lean cuts, such as flank, round or loin. Place the raw meat, fish or poultry on a flat cutting surface. Keep hands, cutting and preparation surface, equipment and utensils clean throughout the jerky-making process. Use a sharp knife to remove as much fat, gristle, membranes and/or tissue as possible. Cut into 1-inch thick pieces. If you cut strips across the grain you will create a jerky that's easier to chew. For a jerky that has more yank, cut with the grain. I cut strips 1/8- to 1/4-inch thick and generally about 5 inches long. The thinner the strips, the faster they dry. Semi-frozen meat is easier to cut than meat at room temperature. If you don't want to do the cutting yourself, have your butcher do it for you. If you use an electric slicer you will get uniform size pieces that should dry in the same amount of time.

MY TERIYAKI STRIP JERKY
1 cup teriyaki sauce
1 teaspoon minced garlic
1/2 teaspoon salt
1/2 teaspoon ground black pepper
1/2 teaspoon liquid smoke

1 pound strips

Mix the ingredients in a bowl, add strips and stir. Marinate at least one hour to give time for the flavors to blend. To marinate longer, cover the bowl and place it in the refrigerator. Remove strips from the marinade and place in a 145 degree drying environment. If any oil beads up during the drying process, pat it off with paper towels. Sometimes jerky needs to be turned over during the drying process so that both sides receive the benefit of the drying air. Let the jerky cool before determining if it's done. When dry, the jerky should bend like a green twig without breaking. Store dry jerky in an airtight container.

SPAM JERKY

Inside the brown envelope with no return address was a sheet of plain white paper. The top line read, "Unforgettable SPAM Jerky." There was no signature. I felt like I'd received a very strange chain letter.

With my curiosity sparked, the next time I went grocery shopping I bought a can of SPAM™ Luncheon Meat. This was just too good to pass up.

My husband said it tasted like the jerky he buys at convenience stores. It may be true that the shelf life is infinite.

UNFORGETTABLE SPAM JERKY

1 12-ounce can of SPAM
3 tablespoons soy sauce
3 tablespoons water
2 tablespoons brown sugar
1 teaspoon Worcestershire sauce
¼ teaspoon fresh horseradish
¼ teaspoon chili powder
¼ teaspoon liquid smoke
as much Scotch bonnet sauce as
    you can handle

Open the can of SPAM and remove. Cut the SPAM into 12 slices. Pile the slices on top of each other and make two more cuts all the way through resulting in 36 pieces.

Put the remaining eight ingredients in a sealable plastic bag. Swish around and add the SPAM slices. Marinate 12 hours to two days in the refrigerator. SPAM is a cooked product; therefore it can be dried at any temperature between 130 and 150 degrees. Do not overlap slices on the drying trays. If any oil appears during the drying process, pat dry with paper toweling. Dry it until chewy, not crunchy.

MAKING GROUND JERKY

Store-bought ground jerky is often referred to as a textured or extruded product. It's usually made with ground beef, or venison, or chicken or turkey that's about 85 percent lean. It is then mixed with various flavorings and dried. There are several good reasons to make ground meat jerky: it takes less time to prepare than the cutting, marinating and handling of strip jerky and there are no leftover scraps of meat. Ground meat absorbs all the marinade, it's cheaper to make, dries faster and is easier to chew. Another bonus of making ground meat jerky is that it is possible to mix various types of meat together—for example you could use half turkey and half beef. Just remember to allow time for the flavorings to blend to get a tasty jerky.

MY GROUND TERIYAKI JERKY

½ cup teriyaki sauce
1 tablespoon olive oil
1 teaspoon minced garlic
1 teaspoon salt
1 teaspoon coarsely ground black pepper
½ teaspoon liquid smoke

1 pound ground meat

Mix the ingredients in a bowl, add the ground meat and thoroughly mix. Wait at least 15 minutes for the flavors to blend. To marinate longer, cover the bowl or put the ground meat mixture in a self-sealing plastic bag and place in the refrigerator.

The challenge of making ground meat jerky is to get the mixture to stick together. That's why it has to be forced.

OPTION 1:
A JERKY GUN OR SHOOTER

A jerky gun or jerky shooter is a gadget that looks like a caulk gun. You fill the chamber with ground meat, pull the trigger and it forces the ground meat into uniform size strips. Generally one pound of ground meat becomes 12 strips that are $3/4$-inch wide and 5 inches long.

OPTION 2:
IF GUNLESS AND SHOOTERLESS

Cold raw ground meat isn't as sticky as meat that is at room temperature. If you moisten your hands with water, the mixture becomes easier to handle. Take one heaping tablespoon of ground meat mixture in your hands and shape it into a ball. Put the ball on top of a piece of waxed paper, then cover it with another piece of waxed paper. With a rolling pin flatten the ball into a $1/4$-inch thick round, then place in a drying environment.

OPTION 3
USE A LOAF PAN

Line a loaf pan with aluminum foil or cellophane wrap. Press the meat mixture into the pan. Put it in the freezer until it's slightly frozen. Remove it from the pan and slice into $1/4$-inch strips, then dry.

OPTION 4

LINE A DEHYDRATOR TRAY

Most food dehydrators have plastic liners that are called Fruit Leather or Roll-up sheets. These plastic liners fit right inside a dehydrator tray. Spoon the ground mixture on the top of a Roll-up sheet. Use a spatula or a wooden spoon or your hands to evenly spread and flatten the mixture so that it's no more than 1/4-inch thick. Place this meat-filled Roll-up sheet on top of a dehydrator tray. Set the temperature at 145 degrees and dry the meat mixture for one hour. Then use a pizza cutter or a serrated knife to make indentations or cut lines that are about one inch apart in the meat mixture. Ultimately these lines will be where the jerky is broken apart to create strips. Return the tray to the dehydrator and dry until the strips can be broken apart at the cut lines. Take the strips off of the roll-up sheets and place them back on the dehydrator tray. By removing the ground meat strips from the Roll-up sheets it makes it easier for air to move around the jerky strips. Continue the drying process. If oil appears on the surface of the drying jerky, pat it off with paper toweling.

When dry, ground meat jerky will bend like a green willow. One pound of ground meat will become about eight ounces of jerky.

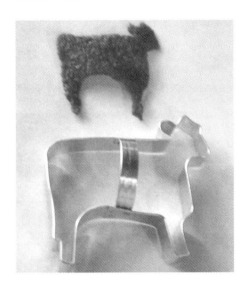

OPTION 5
A PLAYFUL ALTERNATIVE

This is my favorite. Although it is a little more work, it's fun and a good way to get kids involved in making jerky.

Spread a sheet of wax paper on your counter top. Put some of the flavored meat mixture on top

of the wax paper, then put another sheet of wax paper on top of that. Use a rolling pin to flatten the mixture to 1/4-inch thick. Get out your animal shaped cookie cutters. Make impressions in the mixture by pressing the cookie cutters down. Use a deer cookie cutter for ground venison. Use a cow cutter for ground beef.

Carefully lay the animal shape on top of a Roll-up sheet. Dry until it is firm. Remove it from the sheet and put it on a drying tray so that the dry air can get to it more easily. When checking for doneness, make sure the center is completely dry.

DRYING JERKY

Regardless if jerky is dried in a dehydrator, in a smoker, in an attic or in the sun, what is most important is that you can tell when it's finished. Jerky darkens and shrinks when dry. One pound of fresh strips generally becomes a half to a third pound of jerky. To test for doneness, first let the warm jerky cool—warm food always feels softer. Jerky should be flexible enough to bend without breaking, like a green twig. It should not be crisp or brittle. When in doubt, it is safer to over-dry than to under-dry. Jerky must be dried enough so it will not mold. If mold is found in a container of jerky the whole container must be thrown away. Store jerky in an airtight container at room temperature or in the refrigerator or freezer. When packing jerky that feels oily, wrap it in paper towels and let it sit for a couple hours, then remove the oily toweling and reseal. The more airtight the package—the longer the shelf life. The colder the temperature—the longer the shelf life.

TIP: Meat, poultry or fish that's scored dries faster.

DEHYDRATOR

The drying process that fits me best is the food dehydrator. It's so easy to put the soon-to-be-jerky on a tray, turn the dehydrator on and let it go. The time it takes to make jerky depends on the size of strips, the moisture content, the temperature, the humidity in the air, the number of trays on the dehydrator and the wattage of the dehydrator. I use the 1000-watt Gardenmaster dehydrator. I always dry meat at a minimum temperature of 145 degrees. When I prepare eight trays of ground meat jerky it usually takes six to eight hours to dry. With eight trays of strip jerky it takes about eight to 10 hours. If your dehydrator does not have a temperature control, once the jerky seems dry, put it in the oven for 10 minutes at 160 degrees to make sure it is safe to eat.

ATTIC JERKY

Our neighbor, Elton Redalen, is a fifth generation farmer who learned how to make venison jerky from his grandfather who made jerky with his father, and so it went back.

ELTON'S JERKY

2 cups salt

½ cup brown sugar

¼ teaspoon saltpeter

20 pounds venison strips

Combine the dry ingredients, then separate that mixture into thirds. Spread one third of the mixture on ¼-inch venison strips. Put in an earthenware crock and put in a cold environment. Every three days take the strips out of the crock and rub another third of the spice mixture on the strips. On the 12th day remove the strips from the crock and hang them on hangers in a dry, autumn attic for three weeks. This jerky turns black when dry.

AIR DRIED JERKY

Hang a clothesline wherever hot air circulates, either in- or out-doors. Then use clothespins to hold the marinated strips. When drying outdoors, cover the drying strips with cheesecloth to keep insects off.

WOOD STOVE JERKY

Some how figure out how to string a wire in a circle high above a wood stove. Then carefully hang marinated strips over it. Lay a piece of cardboard or newspaper on the floor to catch drips.

DITCH JERKY

Dig a ditch in the side of a hill. Use poles, such as willow branches and build a scaffold over the ditch. Construct this scaffold high enough so it will not catch on fire and yet it will receive the benefit of the fire's smoke. Cover the scaffolding with saplings so it can serve as an oven rack.

Cut meat into long thin strips. Boil a pot of water, add salt, then dip the strips into the boiling water. Place the strips on top of the scaffolding. Make sure they do not touch each other. Build a slow smoky fire in the ditch underneath and keep it going until the jerky is dry.

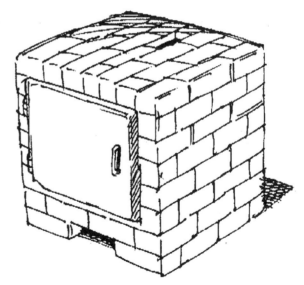

Hickory adds a hearty flavor, especially with red meats and poultry.

Oak is a strong but pleasant hardwood.

Mesquite burns very hot and can turn meat bitter if smoked too long.

Alder has a light delicate flavor and is great for salmon.

Apple and **cherry** produce a slightly sweet, fruity smoke on chicken and turkey.

Pecan is a mellow version of hickory and burns cool.

Others: herb branches or leaves, orange or lemon rinds, grapevines, even corn-cobs are burnable smokey options.

SMOKING

A smoker is a metal container that confines smoke. Inside the smoker are racks or hooks to hang strips so that the smoke can reach all the meat's surfaces. A smoker has a top and bottom draft to efficiently pass the dry air throughout the container. A heat source, such as a hot plate element, is on the bottom. Over the element, a pan holds the material to be used for smoke (various sizes of wood chips, shavings, etc.).

Smokers are always used outside. Smokehouses or smoke ovens can be purchased or built. If you buy one, read the instruction manual.

Clean metal drums, new garbage cans, even old refrigerators have been adapted to be smokers. A smoker can be as simple as erecting a metal foil tent over a hibachi, or as elaborate as building a state-of-the-art brick smokehouse.

Smoking is a drying process. Generally it's the last stage in jerky making. Smoky air is dry. When it hits the jerky strips it adds flavor, promotes good color, evaporates moisture and extends the shelf life. Smoke becomes a film or a protective barrier on the food's surface which can help reduce bacterial and oxidation deterioration. In other words, smoke's antioxidant effect retards the development of rancidity and bacterial growth, thereby providing a preservative effect.

After strips have been dry cured, or brined, or marinated or cooked, they can be either hot or cold smoked. Cold smoking is accomplished between 90 and 120 degrees. It is a curing process that can take days. Hot smoking is generally 160 to 200 degrees and is a short-term, high heat process that usually takes two to six hours. Hot smoking can melt fat and reduce the potential of rancidity in the storing the finished jerky.

Thickness of strips, type of smoke and quantity of food in the smoker can affect the length of the smoking time. High humidity, wind, or cold rainy weather as well as altitude can also impact the amount of time it takes for the smoking process to be completed. During times of high humidity, the moisture released by the drying food may not escape fast enough and the jerky may cook instead of dry.

Because smoke adheres better to a dry surface than a wet one, it is a good idea to put strips in an oven or a dehydrator for an hour or pat them dry using paper towels before putting them in a smoker.

By the way, nuts, cheese, seeds, bread, even table salt can be laid in a thin layer and smoked. Pacific coast natives smoked blueberries. Jalapeno peppers become chipotles after they are briefly put in a smoker.

TIP: Eliminate liquid smoke from your brine or marinade when using a smoker.

TIP: Always lay jerky strips flat in a single layer and do not overlap. Dry air must be able to get to all the surface area.

TIP: Open the smoker lid only when necessary, because every time the lid is lifted you add 15 minutes to the processing time.

KEEP A JERKY-MAKING JOURNAL.

Finally, one last note—jerky-making is a very personal process. Recipes get added to, subtracted from and amended. Keep track of your successes (and failures) in a jerky diary. Just don't lose the key!

Note the weight of the fresh meat, list your flavoring choices and then how long it was marinaded/brined/cured.

Record the type of drying, and if smoking, the type of wood and how long it took to dry.

Jot down ideas on how to adjust your recipe or technique that will better suit your taste in the next batch.

For example, if your jerky is too salty, either decrease the marinating time or reduce the amount of salt. If it is not salty enough, increase the salt and/or the marinating time.

JERKY PEOPLE INDEX

JIM MCGREW

GENTLEMAN JIM'S
GOURMET FOOD
21973 U. S. Highway 19 North
Clearwater, FL 33765
VOICE:
  727-422-0379
WEBSITE:
  www.gentlemanjimsjerky.com

ART OBERTO

OH BOY! OBERTO SAUSAGE
COMPANY
7060 South 238th Street
Kent, WA 98032-2914
Voice 877-234-7904
Fax 877-234-7905
E-MAIL:
  customer.service@oberto.com
WEBSITE:
  www.oberto.com

SEAN BROADNAX

NAX ENTERPRISES
2018 Shattuck Ave, No 17
Berkeley, CA 94704
VOICE:
  510-393-3533
FAX:
  510-272-9463
E-MAIL:
  motherb@mothersjerky.com
WEBSITE:
  www.mothersjerky.com

DEAN CLARK
HI MOUNTAIN JERKY
1000 College View
Riverton, WY 82501
VOICE:
   800-829-2285
FAX:
   307-856-6657
E-MAIL:
   sales@www.himtnjerky.com
WEBSITE:
   www.himtnjerky.com

SANDRO LANE
TAKU SMOKERIES
550 South Franklin Street
Juneau, AK 99801
VOICE:
   800-582-5122
FAX:
   907-463-5312
E-MAIL:
   info@takusmokeries.com
WEBSITE:
   www.takusmokeries.com

MIKE VALLEY
VALLEY FISH SHOP
304 South Prairie Street
Prairie du Chien, WI 53821
VOICE:
   608-326-4719
E-MAIL:
   trapper32@centrytel.net

BILLY HAGBERG
HAGBERG COUNTY MARKET
11325 Stillwater Boulevard North
Lake Elmo, MN 55042
VOICE:
   651-777-2888
FAX:
   651-777-8740

MIKE SCHAFER
SCHAFER FISHERIES
21985 Waller Road
Fulton, Illinois 61252
VOICE:
   815-589-3368
FAX:
   815-589-3369
E-MAIL:
   schafers@cis.net
WEBSITE:
   www.schaferfisheries.com

JUDY LYNCH
DAN LYNCH FARM
214 West Street
Dane, WI 53529
VOICE:
608-8494505
FAX:
608- 850-5049
E-MAIL:
dl@mailbag.com

JACK LINK'S BEEF JERKY
ONE SNACKFOOD LANE
Minong, WI 54859
VOICE:
800-346-6896
FAX:
715-466-5151
E-MAIL:
info@linksnacks.com
WEBSITE:
www.linksnacks.com

LARRY BELITZ
SIOUX REPLICATIONS
HCR-52, Box 176
Hot Springs, SD 57747
VOICE AND FAX:
605-745-3902
E-MAIL:
siouxrep@gwtc.net

STEPHANIE MARCOUX
GRRRMET
3813 179th Place N.E.
Arlington, WA 98223
VOICE:
360-653-2325
FAX:
360-657-2215
E-MAIL:
grrrmet@whidbey.net

LEE HOFER

LEE'S MEAT & SAUSAGES
46754 271st Street
Tea, South Dakota 57064
VOICE:
   888-368-6644
FAX:
   605-368-2161
E-MAIL:
   leesmeats@basec.net
WWEBSITE:
   www.leesmeats.com

KERRY, JACK AND GREGG LOESCH

ARAWAK'S LOBSTER & FISH
MARKET
14301 South Dixie Highway
Miami, FL 33176
VOICE:
   305-235-0501
FAX:
   305-235-2879

RECIPE INDEX

PHOTO CREDITS

Page 4:   HI MOUNTAIN JERKY

Page 7:   *The Seattle Times, Pacific Northwest Magazine*, **January 11, 1998**

Page14:   Rochelle Barnhart

Page 33:   Glenda Ohs

Page 58:   Doug Care Equipment web site

Page 63:   Mary Bell

Page 82:   Taku Smokeries web site

Page 100:   Ira Newman

Page 118:   Mary Bell